# INTERNAL NAVIGATOR
## Basic Steps to Get You from Point A to Point B in Your Life

### THE SECOND EDITION

Dr. Trillion Small

*They Speak Publishing*

Published by They Speak Publishing, Dallas, Texas

Any web address or link contained in this book may
have changed since publication and may no longer be valid.

Headshot photo on back cover by Kauwuane Burton

Printed in the United States of America
ISBN-13: 978-1720288060

# OTHER BOOKS BY DR. TRILLION SMALL

*"Your ears shall hear a word behind you, saying,*
*"This is the way, walk in it,"*
*Whenever you turn to the right hand*
*Or whenever you turn to the left."*
*Isaiah 30:21*

*To my big brother, Dennis Small, Jr.*
*You are a prime example of what is means to handle the "middle*
*stuff" between points A and B well. Continue being the great*
*and determined man that you are. Thanks for always believing*
*in me and protecting me.*
*Love you!*

# TABLE OF CONTENTS

# PREFACE TO THE SECOND EDITION

### HOW THE FIRST EDITION WAS BIRTHED

"The Holy Spirit is like a navigational system; He helps guide you in your life towards destiny." With this simple statement, Bishop Joseph Warren Walker III,[1] planted the seed for me to write the first edition of this book many years ago. My spirit leaped the moment he said it, and I immediately knew I was to expand extensively on that sentence and create a book to help guide others toward purpose.

I was given an awesome, God-inspired idea. Yet the thought of it overwhelmed me a bit. One question consumed my mind: "How will I actually do this; I've never written a book before?" I knew the idea was God breathed, so I wasn't too concerned about *if* it would come to fruition. My concern was on *how* I was going to accomplish it.

Only after I tapped into my own personal navigational system and adhered to the daily guidance of the Holy Spirit was I able to make great strides toward completing my assignment[2] on a daily basis. It was not until I took the necessary first steps that I was able to live on purpose for purpose.

Many of you probably are already well equipped for the road ahead but aren't truly utilizing what you have to its fullest potential. Just because we don't listen to and tap into God's power doesn't mean He isn't there. I was saved when I was seven years old, but it wasn't until I was about twenty that I started paying close attention to my internal navigator, which all believers receive when they accept Jesus Christ as their Lord and Savior.

I knew all along that I had the Holy Spirit within me because I was saved. But I was not fully aware of what an awesome powerful gift and resource He was until I was a junior in college. As I struggled with my choice of a major, I prayed in desperation. After I received the guidance I needed, I began to seek His wisdom for all of my decisions. I soon became much more "Holy Spirit conscious."

Now, the owner of my own counseling and consulting business, an adjunct professor, five books, and a doctorate degree later, I can attest to the importance of having and listening to Holy Spirit. I didn't know it at the time but listening to Holy Spirit means adhering to sound judgment, seeking wise counsel, having prudence and so much more that we will discuss shortly. But most importantly, when you listen to Holy Spirit, you are tapping into Wisdom that you can't Google. Therefore, your internal navigator, your internal Wisdom will lead, guide, and direct you in all areas of your life where you feel stuck, confused, and at a loss for direction. Got Wisdom? I will be utilizing the word *Wisdom* and *Holy Spirit* interchangeably when referencing your internal navigator from here on out.

## WHY A SECOND EDITION

My original reason for wanting to write this book was to share with others what I had learned about living on purpose for purpose and how to obtain our God-given promises. Another reason for writing this book was that there was such a great need for it and many years later, I still see the need. Clients, students, and mentees constantly ask me how to get from where they are to where they desire to go. I believe the journey ahead can be as simple or as complicated as we make it and I desire to help you simplify and fortify your life with this book.

Much of the content from the first edition is the same. I have reorganized, combined and expanded on each chapter, which are now called Steps. I have also created a Facilitators Guide for those who wish to utilize this book in a group setting at their church, school, workplace, or at home with their families. You can find the guide on my website at www.trillionsmall.com.

Also, a new feature of each chapter is called *The Mental and Emotional Health Corner*, *ME Corner* for short. As a mental health clinician, I wanted to be sure that I emphasized the importance of your mental and emotional health along the way. Everything else will be off balance if you have a difficult time regulating and balancing your thoughts and emotions. Take time in the ME Corner and truly allow yourself to be vulnerable and honest when asking yourself, "Is there something within ME that needs to change?" If so, I hope you are willing to take the necessary steps to make those changes so that you can continue on in your journey. I don't know about you, but my ME is very important to me.

I've also added some new topics such as:
- Emotional intelligence
- Psychological hardiness
- Mental clutter extraction
- Journey burnout

I've learned and grown so much since the inception of this book, eight years ago, and I wanted to revive this book with fresh content, fresh revelation, and fresh wisdom. As I reread the first edition, I was delighted to see that many of the principles I believed and practiced then still stand true today. So in your hands you hold a combination of past revelations and fresh wisdom that blend for the perfect recipe.

Rereading this book also reminded me that we all are on and will forever be on a journey in life. There will continue to be new beginnings and endings for us all, so let's take this thing one step at a time together.

# INTRODUCTION

## WHAT I NEED IS INSIDE

Most people know what a navigation system is. Even if you don't own one, you've probably at least seen one. *Internal Navigator* is about the "navigation system" that resides in the innermost part of believers in Christ. I invite you to take a journey with me to discover the basic elements necessary to reach our current "season destination."

In this season of your life, where is God trying to take you? Maybe it's to a deeper relationship with Him. Or perhaps it's toward a physically obtainable goal, such as completing your college coursework and receiving your degree. Whatever it is, the only way you will be successful is if a strategic outline is set forth to prepare the way for you to achieve these accomplishments.

In almost every area of life, a certain course of action must precede the desired outcome. In order to get a job interview, you first need to fill out an application. Before you can take an advanced course, you have to take the prerequisites. To become a judge, you must first be a lawyer. In the same way, if you want to reach the destination God has planned for you, you'll need to submit to certain courses of action first.

How do you know what those courses of action are? The answer will be unique to you. Two people may have the same destination but have completely different pathways to get there. You will know the course of action you need to take by tuning in to your own "internal navigation system." It is personalized just for you. You will reach your divinely appointed destination by allowing God's guiding hand to lead you every step of the way. So turn on your "internal navigation system" and get ready for the ride!

I am excited that you have chosen to become proactive in your life and are choosing to get all that God has for you. As we move through this journey together, I want you to take time to reflect on the Food for Thought questions at the end of each chapter. You may find it beneficial to write down your answers so you can reflect back as you progress toward your destination.

I'm ready. If you are too, let's get going!

## GUIDANCE SIMPLIFIED

"Turn left, bear right, keep straight, sharp turn, make the next legal U-turn…" With so much guidance at our fingertips, it is a wonder how we can go through life and still get lost. Just like with a car's navigational system, the program is only as good as the user who is listening to the instructions.

If you're looking for guidance on how to get from point A to point B in your life, this book is for you. Whether you're seeking help to discover your purpose, looking for assistance on how to finish an assignment or task God has called you to fulfill, or just seeking wisdom on how to live out your purpose, this book is for you too.

Getting from Point A to Point B isn't the problem; it's how we handle what happens in between both points that can lead to stress, confusion, and burnout if mishandled. Throughout this book I will provide you with 7 steps that will help you simplify and fortify your life as you embark on your next journey.

# STEP ONE

## FAMILIARIZE YOURSELF WITH YOUR
## INTERNAL NAVIGATOR

In the 1900s Austrian naturalist Konrad Lorenz carried out one of the first scientific studies for a phenomenon known as *imprinting*. Many young animals (especially birds), upon hatching, will become attached to the first moving object they see. This object may be the animal's mother, a human being, or a ball.

We are born into sin with guaranteed hardships throughout life.[3] From the moment of our birth, we are in a constant struggle between our flesh and our spirit. I believe that is because there are two fathers: the father of all lies, who is satan, and our Heavenly Father, God. Both desire total reign over our souls. But the first "moving object" we see when we are born is satan (or one of his helpers).

That is why Christ said we must be born again; the first imprinting will not suffice. Unless we turn from our wicked ways and become born again, the Kingdom of Heaven will be far from our sight.

Jesus wants us to be reborn so that when we open our eyes this second time we will see, follow, and draw near to Him. Unless you are born again, you will continue to follow your first "moving-object mother," which will lead you away from your destiny instead of toward it. After your rebirth, you will be equipped with the Holy Spirit and ready for your journey.[4]

## TURN ON THE DEVICE

Sounds like a no-brainer, right? But as simple as that step may seem, it is the most important one. If the

17

navigational device isn't turned on, how can you expect to see the route you need to take, begin your journey, or reach your desired destination? It is impossible to accomplish any of this in the Off position. The same is true of having the Holy Spirit but not "turning Him on" (listening to Him).

Let's say you're new in town and a friend gives you a portable navigation system as a gift. You come up with somewhere exciting to go. You know the address. So you hop in the car and throw the navigation device in the glove compartment, still in the box. You start driving, hoping you will end up at the right place.

That's obviously just plain silly. What good is the thing if you leave it in the box? The person who gave you the gift may regret giving you something you refuse to use, especially if you still expect to reach your desired destination.

It's not enough to just receive the gift. You need to do your part to reap the full benefits of it. Although it may seem difficult and frustrating, we must tune in to the guidance of Wisdom. Then get into position, ready to go wherever our Internal Navigator directs us in every aspect of our lives.

There are two sub-categories to *getting into position*. The first is getting into position spiritually and the second is getting into position physically. Getting into position spiritually means to assure that your relationship with Christ is substantial. It means fine tuning your life to be in alignment with His word. Getting into position physically means to be in the right place at the right time and to connect with the right people at the right time. Getting into position spiritually will precede getting into position physically. It takes both to reach your destiny.

# POSITIONING REQUIRES WISDOM

Positioning requires wisdom and in order to have wisdom we must be active listeners. Proverbs 4:5-7 says, "Get wisdom! Get understanding! Do not forget, nor turn away from the words of my mouth. Do not forsake her, and she will preserve you; Love her, and she will keep you. Wisdom is the principal thing; therefore get wisdom. And in all your getting, get understanding" and Proverbs 4:10-15 (MSG) says, "Dear friend, take my advice; it will add years to your life. I'm writing out clear directions to Wisdom Way, I'm drawing a map to Righteous Road. I don't want you ending up in blind alleys, or wasting time making wrong turns. Hold tight to good advice; don't relax your grip. Guard it well—your life is at stake! Don't take Wicked Bypass; don't so much as set foot on that road. Stay clear of it; give it a wide berth. Make a detour and be on your way."

You can get lost in the book of Proverbs reading about Wisdom! It is so rich with revelation and WISDOM but the main thing I want you to take away from these scriptures as it relates to this section of the book is this; wisdom well help you to avoid pointless heartaches, reckless paths, and wasted time! But, it only works if you listen!

Read the entire book of Proverbs 8. Having wisdom helps you have prudence or good sense (v 12), acts as your counselor and helps you to make sound decisions (v 14), and yields blessings and favor (v 32-35). Lacking in any of these areas? Check your Wisdom meter, it may be low.

I understanding how listening to Wisdom can be challenging but I believe it will make more sense as to *how* you can listen if we correlate it with a car's navigational device.[5]

# OPEN YOUR NATURAL EYES AND EARS

When I have my car's navigation system programmed to a certain destination, I find it helpful to both hear and see what it's trying to tell me. If I have my radio on, or someone calls me during my trip, I may miss the verbal directions, but I can easily look at the screen to get a visual picture of what it just instructed me to do. (Of course, I should prevent such distractions, and we will talk about that in Step 2.)

This is how our internal navigator is. The Holy Spirit may speak to us verbally in our mind's eye, but He also speaks to us through circumstances we can see with our natural eyes. These signs may come in the form of a closed or opened door. For example, your boyfriend or girlfriend cheats on you. You lose your job after working with the same company for thirty years. You have many years of education and training, yet you are unable to secure a paid position. Or you have to transfer to a different state for your job, and during the process you connect with someone who can assist you in getting to the next level of your career.

God is trying to tell you something through your circumstances. It isn't a coincidence that you found out that your boyfriend or girlfriend was cheating on you. God may be trying to show you that this man or woman isn't the one for you. If you got laid off from your job, God may have something better for you right around the corner.

## Too Deep for Your Own Good

Many people like getting deeply theological. But sometimes you can get so deep that you miss what God is trying to show you.

Have you heard the joke about the drowning man and the two boats? There are several versions of it but here is the version I heard from a teacher while I was in elementary school:

> One day a man was sailing in the ocean and a storm struck causing his boat to sink. A large boat passed by and the captain said, "Do you need help?" But the man said, "No thanks. God will save me." So the boat left. Soon another large boat came along and the captain said, "Do you need help?" But the man said again, "No thanks. God will save me." So the second boat left. The man ended up drowning. When he got to Heaven, he asked, "God, why didn't You save me?" And God said, "I sent you two boats!"[6]

The moral of the story is that God is almighty and omnipotent, but He can use simple things too. You don't have to watch the sky peel back and God's hand reach down to rescue you in order to see Him move. Many times He operates in still and quiet ways.

A prime example is seen in 1 Kings 19:11–13. When God spoke to Elijah, He wasn't in the strong wind, the earthquake, or the fire, but in the gentle whisper. God may not use huge, elaborate signs to guide us. His direction could be as simple as a whisper.

## OPEN YOUR EYES OF FAITH

The purpose of a car's navigation system is to guide you to your predetermined destination without the help of a map or printed directions. Similarly, the Holy Spirit can direct, guide, and lead us every step of the way. It is tempting, at times, to try to do things our own way, or try to "help" God when we are unable to see how things will work out. With the natural eye, getting to our destination may seem nearly impossible. But "what is impossible with

21

men is possible with God" Luke 18:27 declares. So even if we don't know the route God has planned for our lives, we can rest assured in the knowledge that the Holy Spirit will guide us safely to our divinely appointed destination.

Proverbs 20:24 (NIV) states that "a man's steps are directed by the Lord. How then can anyone understand his own way?" Most of us want to know every detail of the journey. But we need to let go of that idea and rest on the promise that our destination is set and that we will get there one way or another. Before the foundation of the world, God had our lives planned out, and He had everything "worked out in conformity with the purpose of His will."[7]

We should be so convinced about what God has spoken to us that it is apparent in everything we do and say, even if the promise has not yet come to pass in the natural realm. Say what you believe and believe what you say, even if you do not currently see it. Romans 4:17 reminds us to "call those things which do not exist as though they did."

## OPEN THE WORD

Even people who are inexperienced with technology can use automobile navigation systems because they are packaged with user-friendly manuals that provide instructions on how to use them. The Holy Spirit, which we were given at salvation, came with a user-friendly manual too: it's called the Bible.

Shortly after I got my navigation system, I entered a destination that I was already familiar with. But my new high-tech system wanted me to take a route I was unfamiliar with. I wanted to go my usual way instead.

Along our life journey, we may find ourselves in a situation where God's way seems wrong and His timing seems too long. We're tempted to do things our way instead. In times like these, we need to trust that God is guiding us in the right direction. He will never lead us astray. Proverbs 4:12–13 tells us, "When you walk, your steps will not be hindered, and when you run, you will not stumble. Take firm hold of instruction, do not let go; keep her, for she is your life."

Our instruction manual (the Bible) will strengthen our faith as it continuously reminds us that God loves us and He knows what He is doing. It is safe to place our lives in His hands.

## TRACKING DEVICE

Have you ever wondered how a navigation system works? How does it know where you are? And how does it figure out how to get you to wherever you want to go?

Navigation devices use a GPS (global positioning system), which utilizes a cluster of satellites to determine a receiver's location. The device cannot work alone; it has to get signals from a higher power in order to effectively guide you. These satellites also provide your device with your current time and location.

You may feel that you have wandered too far from God. But He knows exactly where you are and He will meet you at the level you are at. He knows whether you are moving or not, and He knows the pace at which you are progressing. No matter what you've done or how far you think you are from God, He knows where exactly you are. Romans 8:38–39 says so.

## FEATURES OF THE SYSTEM

*Gives You What You Need*

Each signal a satellite transmits to a GPS contains a code and prescribed information the receiver uses to determine its position. All of the restaurants, hotels, and gas stations that appear when you click "Near City" will be close to the location you are currently in. If you're in Arkansas, your device will not give you information pertaining to Arizona.

Your Internal Navigator works the same way. The Holy Spirit will not give you insight into a situation if you are not at a spiritual level that enables you to receive it. Most of the time He shows us the next step we need to take. He rarely shows us the end result. My guess is that if He showed us the entire process, most of us would quit before we got started, because all that information would be too much for us to handle in our immature state. He knows the amount of revelation to share with us in each stage we are in. He will send a *rhema* word[8] into our path to speak to us in our current season.

Whatever you need, God can give it. If victory is what you need, call on Jehovah Nissi. If healing is what you need, call on Jehovah Rapha. If you're not sure what you need, call on the great I AM.

*Always at Your Disposal*

Your car's navigation system receives information from satellites on a continuous basis. So it offers access twenty-four hours a day, seven days a week, 365 days a year. However, this guarantee is only applicable to those who are properly equipped. If you do not have a navigation device, you obviously won't receive any satellite information.

If you don't have the Holy Spirit, or you are not allowing the Spirit to control your life, there is no way you can properly receive a word from the Lord. The flesh does not understand things in the spirit realm (I Corinthians 2:6-16). But the Holy Spirit is available to all believers, any time of the day or night.

Fortunately for travelers, a GPS is not affected by weather. And God's ability to move in our lives is not contingent upon what is going on around us. If He wants to move in our lives, He can no matter rain, hail, sleet, snow, hurricane, or sunshine.

We don't need to wait until the storm is over. We can praise God *in* it. Because storms do not affect the Holy Spirit's ability to provide guidance to us. Even during the toughest times, the Holy Spirit that dwells within you can give you the tugs and pulls you need to get you through.

TIMING DIFFERENCE

I find it amazing that my car's navigation device can be hundreds of miles away from the satellites embedded in the transmitted radio signal, yet the time on my device's clock is never off.

Your timing (chronos) and God's timing (Kairos) sometimes seem very different. But the Holy Spirit makes sure everything happens right on time. We may feel like He'll never make the changes in our lives we want. But He knows just the right time to show up and we can rest assured that He may not come when we want Him, but He will always be on time! (We will discuss timing more in Step 5.)

IMPORTANT FACTORS TO CONSIDER

Before I upgraded to a car with a built-in navigation system, I had one of those GPS devices you buy from the store that sticks to the windshield. The little suction cup was hard for me to take off my window, so I soon stopped using it. Whenever I needed the device, I held it in my hand or placed it under my radio.

When I held it in my hand, it seemed to take forever for the thing to boot up. I got tired of reading "searching for signal" on the screen. I tried moving it to different areas of my car to see if that would help. The closer I got it to the windshield, the sooner it found a signal.

Then one day I read something interesting in an online manual about navigation systems. "From any location on or near the earth, a GPS receiver with an unobstructed view of the sky should be able to track at least four satellites, thereby being able to calculate the receiver's precise latitude, longitude, and elevation."[9] A navigation system works best when it is in a position that's clear of distractions or blockages.

We work the exact same way. We are at our best when we have minimal distractions (more about this in Step 2) and when we're in the right position to hear clearly from the Holy Spirit (more about this in Step 3).

I also read in this manual that "the GPS receiver performs filtering and generates positioning data to be outputted to a navigation device and the like."[10] The more time we spend with the Lord, experiencing Him and learning about Him, the better we will be able to distinguish His voice. (I highly recommend a book titled *Two Chairs* by Bob Beaudine if you want to strengthen your ear to hear God.)

Along life's journey, we hear many voices, get many opinions and suggestions, and see many things. We need to filter out the "junk mail" so we have room to store worthwhile mail in our "inbox."

First Thessalonians 5:21 (NIV) tells us to "test everything. Hold on to the good." Take time to read God's Word, pray, fast, serve, fellowship, etc. so you will be able to determine what is good and what is not.

Sometimes in life, though, some "not so good" things happen and it can steal our hope and joy. Check out The Mental and Emotional Health Corner as I talk more about hope.

| **Mental and Emotional Health Corner** |
| --- |

### HOPE KEEPS US GOING

One of the main functions of the video display on a navigational system is to show users their desired routes via a map. This map shows where the vehicle needs to travel to get to the destination. My system offers an option to "View Entire Route." This gives me a "virtual tour" of the journey before I start driving. Pretty neat, right?

The Holy Spirit won't take you on a "virtual tour" of your entire route. But from time to time He does allow us to see some of the path ahead, our progress along that path, and even our final destination. He may show us these things in the natural realm by opening and/or closing specific doors. Or by having us to simply look back and see how much we have changed and how far we have come. He may also show us these things in the spiritual realm by allowing someone to give us a prophetic word about the journey, revealing it to us in a vision or dream, or speaking directly to us through a sermon. But either way, these glimpses strengthen our faith and keep hope alive while we're on the journey.

I know the road may get tough, lonely, and discouraging but one thing that helps me to hold on is HOPE! I often tell my clients, especially those who are depressed or suicidal, that it is important to always have something to look forward to in the future. Whether that be a lunch date with a friend, an upcoming event, or a personal project that has a nearing deadline. What ever it is, it must be something that you can wake up and look forward to. When we stop pursing things for our future we can become complacent and docile. And when that happens, we have lost hope. And when we lose hope; we lose focus. And when we lose focus we forget the meaning and the why of life. Feeling hopeless? Plan something exciting a couple of weeks out and continue doing that on a regular basis.

Take time to read the two scriptures below. Disappointments do make our hearts sad but rest assured in knowing that God has a plan to give you hope and future. So keep hope alive! It's what makes you try one more time.

**"Hope deferred makes the heart sick, but a longing fulfilled is a tree of life." Proverbs 13:12 (NIV)**

**"For I know the plans I have for you," declares the LORD, "plans to prosper you and not to harm you, plans to give you hope and a future." Jeremiah 29:11 (NIV)**

## ✠ *Food For Thought* ✠

1. Read 1 Corinthians 3:16 and 6:19-20.
   a. What does it mean to you to have the Holy Spirit living inside you?
2. How do you think you can honor God with your body?
3. Now that you know the Holy Spirit dwells inside of you, what do you think His purpose is there? What type of things do you think He will do in and through you?
4. Read Acts 2:38. How does it feel to be given such a gift? Do you consider it special and valuable, or something you were given and aren't too crazy about (like that ugly sweater from your great aunt)?
5. Read Romans 8: 11.
6. The Spirit that raised Jesus from the dead is the same Spirit that can give you life. What does this mean to you?

# STEP TWO

## ADDRESS ANY DISTRACTIONS AND BARRIERS BEFORE GETTING STARTED

Take this book and bring it up to your nose. Now take the book away from your face. What did you see each time? The closer the book was to your face, the less of your surroundings you could see, and the farther the book was from your face, the more of your surroundings you could see.

To minimize the many distractions around you, zoom in your focus on the things that are important: getting into your purpose and fulfilling God's will for your life. You can also call this "tunnel vision": focusing on the end result and not on the surrounding environment. It's not that you lack awareness of the circumstances and roadblocks around you; rather, you decide not to allow temporary tribulations to hinder your permanent promises.

### MINIMIZE DISTRACTIONS

*The Past*

Focus becomes counterproductive when our gaze is in the wrong direction. Our past mistakes, failures, and pains often are one of our biggest distractions. The emotions attached to our past adverse experiences can feel so real that it pulls our attention away from the present and robs us of our future. There is a story in Genesis 19 about a guy named Lot, his wife, and his two daughters. They were instructed to leave their town and not turn back. But while they were fleeing the city, Lot's wife looks back and turns into a pillar of salt. Feeling a little salty lately? Feeling a litter bitter and resentful about things that have happened in your life? If so, this is a prime indicator that your gaze is in the past and not in your future. Turn your head back around and refocus your attention on what is ahead of you instead of on what is behind you.

*Self*

Not only can your past get in the way, but you can get in your own way too. Many times, as I've been driving to a specific place, I ended up missing my exit or turn. The signs were there, no other cars were in my way, and there were no unusual circumstances, such as road construction or a change in the weather, that hindered my view. I missed my turn because I was not focused on where I was going. My body was in the car, but my mind was somewhere else. Because I was not focusing on the task at hand, I missed my exit.

We become our worst enemies when we get in the way of our own selves. We are to "love the Lord with all of our heart and with all of our soul and with all of our mind and with all of our strength."[11] But how can we please Him if we are not totally present as we're doing what He has asked of us?

We wouldn't want to purchase an automobile that was missing a tire or an engine, because a car needs all of its parts (seen and unseen) to function properly. God wants us to be fully equipped and fully engaged.

One of the most important factors of being an effective counselor is to be fully present with the client. People can tell when you are daydreaming and not truly focusing on the things they are saying. One clear indication is that you are unable to repeat back the statement they just made.

Have you ever stopped talking to ask someone, "Are you listening to me?" Something about that person's demeanor made you feel like he or she wasn't paying attention. So you shut down without even finishing your thought.

Imagine how the Holy Spirit feels when He's speaking to our hearts and we say we're listening but our demeanor says otherwise.

We have to empty our minds and remove the clutter of our busy day so we can be fully present with the Holy Spirit and hear all the things He wants to share with us. If our minds are somewhere else while we're "driving," we probably won't reach our destination in a timely manner because we'll miss God's directions and ignore His important warnings and instructions.

God got very upset when Israel stopped listening to Him. Let us not do the same. Don't allow your distracted mind to hinder you from receiving guidance and instruction from the Holy Spirit. Take the time to do what I call a *Mental Clutter Extraction*.

Sometimes it doesn't even take a person or a circumstance to set us back. The things that go on between our two ears often are enough. What irrational, unhealthy, and unhelpful thoughts do you have that are literally cluttering the pathways of your mind? Do you often think that you are a failure, or that you aren't good enough, or that you don't have what it takes, or that people won't show up and support you? Do you often ruminate on the worst-case scenario? Why?

I find it fascinating that our minds are more likely to dwell on all that could go WRONG instead of what could go RIGHT! The next time you have thoughts like, what if this doesn't work, what if they reject me, what if I'm not chosen, or what if this goes wrong, I want you to instead command your mind to shift and instead say, what if this works, what if they accept me, what if I'm chosen, what if this goes exactly the way I had in mind or better? Do you see how the second set of questions make you smile and feel so much better about life and about your journey?

As you can see, our own mental and emotional state can get in our own way. Check out The Mental and Emotional Health Corner to see if you have any of the listed conditions that are barriers to your journey. Each of these shut your ear to Wisdom thus stifles your progress. It's like muting the volume of your GPS and turning the display screen off. You simply end up stuck and/or lost.

| The Mental and Emotional Health Corner | |
|---|---|
| Prideful/Stubbornness | Metaphorically speaking, pride and stubbornness are like having earplugs in your ear all while the building fire alarm is going off but you never hear it because of your unwillingness to take the earplugs out. Each is a self-destructive trait that can lead to your own downfall if not careful. Elevating yourself to the point where you idolize yourself and the works of your own hands is a dangerous road to travel. |
| Unforgiveness | I image unforgiveness to be like stabbing your own heart and waiting for the person who hurt you to bleed. Forgiveness not only frees the other person from a penalty that they may rightfully deserve but it also frees you to move on with your life and not be |

| | |
|---|---|
| | chained by the past. While you may feel like you have control by not letting go of what they did, you are basically holding on to your breath but expecting to live. It doesn't work. Could your unforgiveness be the barrier preventing you from the next level? I know it was for me personally. |
| Hard-hearted | Unforgiveness leads to a hard heart. God looks at the condition of our heart as He prepares to launch us to the next level. Could the hardness of your heart be weighing and slowing down your elevation process? You know that you have a hard heart when you are apathetic, unloving, often angry, and have low compassion. You know you have a soft heart when you are caring, kind, gentle, empathetic, compassionate, and loving. |

*Relationships*

Family, Friends, and Foes

When you're planning a road trip with several people, you seriously consider who is going to ride where. If you're like me, you want the annoying people in a different car from yours, and the fun people with you in your car.

When driving to our preordained destination, we have a few choices for the riders who will accompany us. I divide these people into four categories: the frequent stoppers, the complainers, the sleepers, and the participators.

## Frequent Stoppers

These are the people who always have to go to the bathroom, are always hungry or thirsty for something that's not in the car, or feel the need to stop at every store. These people will delay you from getting to your destination, because they can always find something more important to do than getting to where you need to be.

If this person is you, I'd like to suggest that your excuses for delaying the progress of your journey come from fear, which has been implanted in you by the enemy, saying things like "You will never make it; you might as well stop now" and "No one has ever done what you're trying to do; what makes you think you will succeed at it?" and "Look at your parents. They couldn't get there, and you're in the same family, so you won't either." The enemy tries to implant these thoughts in our minds to get us off track.

Frequent stoppers in your life's journey will do the same. They will see your efforts as you pursue your destiny and will directly or indirectly try to slow your progress. So rather than respecting that you are busy over the weekend working on some things God has told you to do they will instead try to sway you from doing them. They don't want to get left behind but instead of catching up they try to slow you down.

## Complainers

Complainers are never satisfied, no matter what you try to do to please them. The car's too hot or too cold, the music is too loud or too soft, you're driving too fast or too slow, their legs are cramped, their backs hurt from sitting so long, and on and on and on. These people may not slow your process, but they will annoy and frustrate you, making your journey very unpleasant.

Complainers are always bugging you with questions. "Why do you have to do that?" Even if you're sure you are doing the right thing, they complain about what you are or aren't doing. And they're not exactly thrilled about your successes. "Look at her. She thinks she's better than everyone else 'cause she has ..." In truth, they are so upset about their unproductive, fruitless lives, they want to drag everyone else into their pity party.

Sleepers

Sleepers always take but never give. They offer no assistance in driving, no conversation to keep you alert enough to keep going. They are unaware of all that took place on the ride. All they care about is the end result ... and reaping the benefits without having to put in any work.

En route to your destination, you will need someone to motivate you, to push forward, to encourage you to see it through to the end, and to bear your load for a while if it gets too heavy.

The ride to your destination is not guaranteed to be a smooth, straight shot. So you need someone to come along on the ride who is motivated and driven. You don't want someone else's laziness or lack of effort to rub off on you until you become too content to continue on. "A little sleep, a little slumber, a little folding of the hands to rest— and poverty will come on you like a thief and scarcity like an armed man" (Proverbs 6:10-11).

Participators

Participators offer good conversation along the way and check on you often to make sure you're doing okay. If you get too tired to drive, they volunteer to pitch in. These people experience every moment of the ride with you.

Participators "bear one another's burdens, and so fulfill the law of Christ."[12] I like the participators, because they make you feel like you're not alone. If you get a little weary, they'll build you up so you have the strength to go on. They're not spectators, who sit back and watch, but active participators who are genuinely interested in getting you to your destination safely.

If you get a little tired along the way, they will pray for you, interceding on your behalf. When you feel like giving up, they hold you accountable to make sure you keep your focus and don't get side-tracked by other things. They will be your extra set of ears in case you fail to hear an instruction given by your Internal Navigator. These people don't have a problem with gently reminding you what the Lord has said concerning your life.

-----------------

You may be thinking, *Sounds like I'll have to kick everybody out the car and drive solo.* There may be times along your journey when you will have to go it alone. Everybody can't go with you to your destination. Some people you'll need to drop off and some you will need to pick up along the way.

Don't get bogged down by the number of passengers in your car. And don't get discouraged if you see someone else's car full of people, seemingly having fun, while yours is empty. You may be in a season of isolation. Use those times of aloneness to draw closer to God.

Many people associate being alone with being lonely. But they are not the same thing. Being lonely is when you desire company but don't have it. Being alone acknowledges the lack of company but embraces the opportunity to spend time with oneself.

Time alone enables you to rid yourself of distractions. It also allows you to reflect on your life and question the things you're doing. When you are alone, you don't have anyone to talk to, so you have to talk to yourself.

David had some great time alone. In Psalm 43:5, we see him talking to himself. *Why are you cast down, O my soul? And why are you disquieted within me? Hope in God; for I shall yet praise Him, the help of my countenance and my God.*

You don't need to climb the highest mountain to find your place of solitude. Simply reach into your life when you are able to free yourself of external influences and opinions, and reflect on the Word of God and whatever matters are concerning you. Consider this your "me time."

There was a moment in Samuel's life when God was trying to speak to him, but he was so busy running back and forth he didn't recognize the voice calling him. However, Eli realized it was God. So he told Samuel to go lie down, and if he heard his name called again, to respond, "Speak, Lord, for your servant hears" (I Samuel 3: 1-10).

We all need people in our lives who will tell us to go sit down somewhere! Busyness does not equal productive progress. Go somewhere quiet for a while and listen to what God has to say to you.

------------------

Remember, the longer the trip and the more people you have, the more baggage you will have to tote around! If any passengers do not respect your destiny enough to push you toward it, make a quick pit stop and let them out. You don't need to carry around unnecessary weight. The heavier the load, the more gas you burn, and purposeless weight gets expensive.

It may hurt initially to lose a load or two. But when the pain ends, you'll realize it was worth your while. I don't want anybody in my car who doesn't offer encouraging words or support to press forward.

------------------

Judges 7 reminds us that life is not so much about the number of people around us but the quality of those people. In verse 2, the Lord said to Gideon, "You have too many men. I cannot deliver Midian into their hands, or Israel would boast against me, 'My own strength has saved me.'" Then the Lord told him how to lessen the number of men. He did this twice, taking him from thirty-two thousand to twenty-two thousand and finally only three hundred. A whole lot of people were cut from Gideon's entourage.

It's okay to build a team of people to help you accomplish whatever you're trying to do. But don't let a board become a replacement for God's working in your life.

Significant Others

Those we choose to date and/or marry could be another relational distraction. "Can two walk together, unless they are agreed?" (Amos 3:3). You may have a significant other who is cute, good at conversation, have it all together, and may even be "good" people, but they aren't saved, or they're not living like they are. These relationships can make you feel like you're living, but spiritually you are dying.

If you have a significant other who isn't living for God and striving to be more like Him daily, you can't expect him or her to hold you accountable when it comes to going about your Kingdom business. Slowly but surely your convictions will diminish, sinning won't hurt as much, and your boundaries will dissipate. Your destination will become distorted because your significant other is unable to offer you a correct perspective. You will follow his or her ways of life and get off track. Then you'll be wondering how you ended up in that predicament.

When you get into a hot tub, you have to ease your way in: a toe, then a foot, then your legs, and then the whole body. Once you're in for a period of time, your body becomes accustomed to the hot water. If you stay in long enough, your skin will lose elasticity (evidenced by the wrinkles on your hands and feet).

The same principle applies when you step into a "hot relationship." It is uncomfortable in the beginning, and you know you have no business being in it. But inch by inch you ease your way in until you become comfortable. If you submerge yourself in this "hot" situation for too long, you will become weaker. Your walk will no longer have that firm stance you had before. Instead of becoming more like Christ, you look more like the world.

You can't expect to play with fire and not get burned (see Proverbs 6:27).

*Noise*

"Turn the music down. I can't see!" I know that statement doesn't make logical sense. But whenever I'm driving to an unfamiliar place, or doing something difficult like parallel parking, I can't focus on my task if there's blaring music or if people are talking to me. What we hear ultimately affects what we see.

Have you ever looked at one of those optical illusion pictures, where different people see the same image as different things? One person might see two heads facing

41

each other, while another person sees a cup or vase. Which one you see is often determined by what someone told you the picture was.

Who is talking to you in your life? Whatever they tell you will affect how you see your situations.

External noise, such as music and talking, can drown out the voice of the navigation system, making it difficult for you to hear where you are supposed to go next. If you can't hear the instructions, you won't be sure where to go. You may see the arrow on the screen, but you won't know whether you need to turn immediately or wait another block. Turning too early or too late could make a big difference.

Some people complain that God isn't guiding them clearly. He is speaking. But those people have so much noise going on in their lives, they are unable to hear His soft whispers. We have to just tune some people out. Turn down the negative volume and turn up the positive volume so you can hear and see where God wants you to go.

## REGAIN FOCUS

On this journey called life, we are guaranteed trouble. When trials come, we need to remove the distracting elements in order to regain our focus. This process isn't easy. But with a great deal of attention, some alone time, and a few attitude adjustments, you will be able to put your focus back on getting into position and fulfilling your purpose.

### Selective Attention

Scientific studies have proven that people cannot focus on several stimuli all at once. We must tune out some things in order to focus on others. For example, if you're at a party with loud music and several conversations going on around you, you have to choose which sound you want to hear. Or if you're on the phone and someone else is talking to you, you will miss what one of those people is saying because you can't process both at the same time. This is called selective attention (otherwise known as the "cocktail party effect").[13]

One of my college buddies is a pro at selective attention. On several occasions when we've gone out to eat together, I've been in the middle of telling him something and suddenly noticed him engulfed in another table's conversation. He's managed to tune out my voice, and the restaurant's background music, and hear everything the group across from us is saying. I always tease him when I catch him doing that, telling him he might as well join that table.

This same concept applies to us. We need to minimize distractions in order to focus on what God is saying. The enemy never stops talking in our ears, attempting to derail us. But he cannot stop us from hearing God if we choose to focus on His voice.

A unique facet of selective attention is that if you have two different sound stimuli in each of your ears at the same time, you will only be able to pay attention to the sound in one of your ears. The sound in the other ear will not be received consciously.

If the Holy Spirit is whispering in your right ear and the enemy in your left, you need to decide which ear to pay attention to. The enemy may be screaming at the top of his lungs to get your attention. But if you have chosen the right ear, you will be able to pay attention to the Holy Spirit, and the enemy's nonsense will be irrelevant.

Focusing on God has to be a conscious decision. He won't force you to listen to Him. He will keep talking whether you have that ear "turned on" or not.

Allow Christ to capture your full attention, and block out anything that is speaking the opposite of what you know to be true.

*Release Some Things*

The act of vomiting is never pleasant. However, shortly after the release, you usually feel much better. Your stomach was letting you know that something inside you was making you sick. If you didn't release it, you would only feel worse.

Some people and situations can make us sick—physically, mentally, emotionally, or spiritually—if we hold on to them. You may rationalize that holding on would be better for you because you don't want to let go. The guy or gal you're with doesn't treat you right. You tolerate the behavior because you think life without this special person is impossible. But that individual is making you sick by devaluing you. The longer you hold on to this relationship, waiting for it to change, the worse your condition will get. If you release this person, the sickness will subside.

------------------

I stopped by my friend's work one day, just to say hi. While I was there, one of his former employees came in and asked for some advice about a relationship she was in. Since we were both prospective counselors, we offered to help. The young lady told us she'd recently broken up with a guy but wasn't over him yet, and now an old friend wanted to date her. When I asked her why this was a problem, she said that although the bad things about the first boyfriend outweighed the good, she was afraid she might never find those few good things again.

44

I assured her that her feelings were not out of the ordinary. I then told her how I had managed to get over someone who had hurt me by reminding myself that God had released me from harmful situations before, so I knew He could do it again. Each time I let go of those "few good things," I received more good things the next go-around.

With every release of whatever you're holding on to, life gets better. God has so much more in store for you if you will only let go of what you have.

If you get bit by a poisonous snake, you need to have the venom sucked out of the wound. If you get chemicals in your eye, you need to rinse it for a period of time. Sucking out venom and putting water in your eyes are not pleasant things to do. But they're necessary in order to remove whatever is hurting you and to prevent further harm. Similarly, letting go is never fun or easy, but it is essential to preserve your life and to function properly.

Maybe what you're struggling to release is not a relationship or a person. Maybe it's a drug. Or an unproductive habit, such as cursing, viewing porn, or visiting places that cause you to stumble or be greatly tempted. Perhaps you need to forgive yourself for bad things you've done in the past, or forgive others who have hurt you. In order to move forward, you have to release yourself from guilt and shame, and release others from having control over your thoughts and feelings.

Once you've let go of those things that are harmful to your destiny, and gained a better awareness and focus, you will be ready to make the necessary preparations of fulfilling your purpose.

## ✠ *Food For Thought* ✠

1. "Do not be deceived: evil company corrupts good habits." (1 Corinthians 15:33)
   a. Why is it important to carefully choose the people you allow into your life?
2. How do the people in your life now influence you (both positively and negatively)?
3. Are there some people in your life who should not be? Who and why?
4. What are some distractions in your life? How can you minimize them?
5. "Teach me your way, Lord, that I may rely on your faithfulness; give me an undivided heart, that I may fear your name." (Psalm 86:11 NIV)
   a. What does it mean to have an undivided heart?
   b. Pray this Psalm and ask the Lord to help you to manage all of the distractions in your life that have been hindering you from pursuing God wholeheartedly. Make a commitment today to no longer allow things (or yourself) to stand in the way of receiving what God has for you.
6. Is what you are holding on to worth being sick over?

# STEP THREE

## IDENTIFY YOUR POINT A: WHERE ARE YOU NOW?

### KNOW YOUR PART

I remember October 31, 2012, like it was yesterday. I was in a theatrical play and I was the new actress on set. I guess I had the call time wrong, because when I arrived for our first performance, the show had already started. That was a major dilemma for me, because I didn't know my lines!

Fortunately for me, the other players on stage gave me cues as to when it was my turn and told me what to say. Amazingly, this worked quite well.

However, speaking lines wasn't my only job. There was also a dance segment, and I didn't know that either. While I waited backstage, I asked my fellow dancers to show me how to do the steps. They told me I didn't have to do the dancing part, but I was insistent, so they showed me the moves. The routine wasn't difficult and I caught on fairly quickly. Still, I didn't want to mess up, so I asked them to help me practice.

While we were rehearsing backstage, the director passed by and I stopped him. Waving the script in the air with bit of an attitude, I whispered, "Did you know that I didn't get one of these?"

He just looked at me and said, "Yes".

I was so stunned, I couldn't think of anything to say back. I just stood there with my hands on my hips.

After the performance, I expected to get some kind of recognition for how well I did despite the fact that I did not have the script prior to the show. But the director didn't say a word to me!

At that point, I woke up and realized this was only a dream. Thank goodness!

## BE A GOOD STEWARD OF WHAT YOU ALREADY HAVE AND KNOW

My entire life I've been a planner and a perfectionist. I like to know what is about to happen and what will follow. I'm one of those people who create to-do lists with little boxes next to each item so I can check them off. Just "going with the flow" and waiting to see what happens is not my style.

At the time when I had this dream, I was always asking God, "Okay, Lord, after I do this, what's next?" I wanted a step-by-step itinerary well ahead of time. But that wasn't happening. I had a goal of writing a book, and I knew what I had to do: write a business plan, come up with an "elevator pitch," prepare a book proposal, record my vision for the book. I was okay with all that because I knew they needed to be done. But I wanted to know more.

I repeatedly asked God for detailed instructions, but He never gave them. Finally I decided to start on the first step: my business plan and book proposal. To my amazement, the moment I started writing those things, I began getting guidance on the next step. God wanted me to act on what I already knew before He was willing to give me more.

---

If you are stuck in an idle place and struggling to make foreword progress, here are a few factors to consider:

*Total Trust*

If you want more, show God that you honor what He has already given you. Prove to Him that He can trust you by displaying your full trust in Him with every aspect of your life—the known and the unknown.

The message God wanted to get across to me in that dream is that I am not going to know every single detail about the tasks He calls me to do. Some things I won't know how to do, but He will teach me. Sometimes I won't know what to say, but when it is time, He will give me the words to speak.

In my dream, I didn't know anything about the production, yet the show turned out to be a huge success. I didn't blow it or make a fool of myself. That is what God is saying to us corporately. When He has called us to do something, He will equip us to fulfill it. And He has already made provisions for it to be a success. It is our duty to trust Him wholeheartedly, let Him guide our every step, and not allow fear to hinder us.

Fear is a key component to stagnation, and it has the ability to keep us stuck in a place so we never reach our full potential. If we totally trust God, we will be like a little child who leaps into her daddy's arms, knowing he will catch her and not let her fall.

Have you totally surrendered to God? Do you trust Him with all of your cares?

*Drop the Entitlement Mind-set*

In my dream, I thought it odd that the director did not comment on my good performance. I had done well, and I knew he saw me, so I was looking for some sort of "Good job," a pat on the back, or a "Wow, you did it!" Something that let me know he acknowledged my good work. There is nothing wrong with wanting praise when you do something great. But you may not get any acknowledgment for doing what you're supposed to do.

When you were a child, you may have been praised for putting your clothes and shoes on all by yourself. But as an adult you shouldn't expect to receive that same recognition because you should know how to do all that. You don't get accolades from your boss for showing up to work on time every day. If you walked into your boss's office every morning and stood in his doorway with your hands on your hips, saying, "It's eight AM; I'm here on time," he would look at you like you were crazy.

God doesn't have anything against applauding us for a job well done. But some things are simply expected of us, such as trusting God every step of the way. So a pat on the back may not follow every faith-taking step we make.

Four months after that dream, I came across a passage in the Gospels that backed up the interpretation I already had. Here is how *The Voice* translates it:

*Imagine this scenario. You have a servant—say he's been out plowing a field or taking care of the sheep—and he comes in hot and sweaty from his work. Are you going to say, "You poor thing! Come in and sit down right away"? Of course not! Wouldn't you be more likely to say, "First, cook my supper and set the table, and then after I've eaten, you can get something to eat and drink for yourself"? And after your servant has done everything you told him to do, are you going to make a big deal about it and thank him? [I don't think so!] Now apply this situation to yourselves. When you've done everything I'm telling you to do, just say, "We're servants, unworthy of extra consideration or thanks; we're just doing our duty." (Luke 17:7–10)*

## DO YOUR PART

For the most part, I am a visual person when it comes to learning and memorization. I have to write Scriptures and words of inspiration on a sticky note or on my bedroom mirror with a dry erase marker if I want them to stick in my head.

Currently on my mirror I have three columns written. The first column is "My Part," the second is "Scripture," and the third is "God's Part." Isaiah 26:3 is the first Bible verse on the list. According to this, "My Part" is to keep my mind on the Lord and trust Him, while "God's Part" is to keep me in perfect peace.

We will never accomplish what we need to do if we are more worried about someone else's part than our own. Could you imagine how much of a mess we would be in if our legs didn't want to do their job of carrying us from point A to point B? What if they decided they wanted to be eyes? It is good to be ambitious and strive for success. But in the midst of your planning, do not forget the one who is determining your steps (Proverbs 16:9).

Maybe you're not the type of person who tries to jump the gun and do things that don't concern you. Perhaps you're the kind of person who doesn't do anything at all.

One of my classmates once told me, "I can sit in my closet all day and pray that God will give me a hot dog. But if I don't get up and begin searching for places where I can find one, I'll never get it." You can pray all you want for something to happen, but what are you doing after you get off your knees?

"Lord, help me find a job," you plead. Yet you haven't filled out any applications. "Lord, help me to lose weight," you whine. But the fried chicken joint counts your money daily. The Lord is waiting for us to do our part before He does His part.

Some Scripture promises have conditional conjunctions, such as *if, then,* and *unless.* For example, 2 Chronicles 7:14 tells us that *if* we humble ourselves, pray, and seek His face, and turn from our wicked ways, *then* He will hear from Heaven and forgive our sins and heal our land. After we do our part to the best of our ability, we can watch God step in and do what we can't.

God isn't going to do for you what you can do yourself. Before Jesus left this earth, He told the disciples to go forth and heal the sick, cast out demons, raise the dead, and cleanse the lepers. He didn't say, "Pray to God and ask Him to do those things for you." He told them to do them because He told them they could.

-----------------

## GOT ACTION?

So often we get caught up in trying to rush through steps to get to the finished product, but we must remember that our God is a God of order, and since everything He does is decent and in order, what we do should be too.[14]

You may feel like you're stuck and you don't know what you should do next. But my guess is that you do know what you should be doing now. You just have to decide that laziness, mediocrity, and complacency are no longer options for you. You must rid yourself of all excuses, especially the one that says, "I'm waiting on God to do it."

Getting to our destiny requires a collaborative effort between you and God. He speaks the promise and you move toward that promise as He makes continual provisions along the way.

Those who have the mind-set that says, "If God wants it done, He will do it Himself," will seldom reach their full potential and obtain all of God's promises for them. God requires some level of action from us. If you don't believe me, just look at Moses, Gideon, and Jesus. Moses had to lift up his rod and stretch out his hand over the Red Sea to divide it (Exodus 14:16). Gideon had to arise and go down to the camp of Midian in order for it to be delivered into his hands (Judges 7:9). Jesus had to come into the world to do the will of God and finish His work so that we might be saved (John4:34 and John 3:17). These are a few examples of actions that had to be taken in order for God's will to be fully established.

*Are You Planting or Watering?*

The first step toward knowing what to do is to understand your role.

*1 Corinthians 3:4–10*

*For when one says, "I am of Paul," and another, "I am of Apollos," are you not carnal? Who then is Paul, and who is Apollos, but ministers through whom you believed, as the Lord gave to each one? I planted, Apollos watered, but God gave the increase. So then neither he who plants is anything, nor he who waters, but God who gives the increase. Now he who plants and he who waters are one, and each one will receive his own reward*

53

*according to his own labor. For we are God's fellow workers; you are God's field, you are God's building. According to the grace of God which was given to me, as a wise master builder I have laid the foundation, and another builds on it. But let each one take heed how he builds on it.*

Each person has a part to play in life, whether it be planting or watering. Knowing our roles will alleviate unnecessary stress and strain. If you are meant to plant but instead you choose to water, you are wasting your time and resources, pouring water where there is no seed. If you are supposed to water but instead choose to plant, you are doing steps that have already been done and therefore hindering the growth of the seed due to a lack of nurturance and care. If you are not planting or watering as you are meant to, but simply trying to make increase, you are trying to fill a role under your own power.

Only God can give increase. So you don't have to suck up to anybody or sell your soul to get noticed or promoted. Promotion comes from God, not man.[15] Know your part, do your part, and let God do the rest.

## WHOSE WILL IS IT ANYWAY?

In order to do what God has called you to do, you need to know what His will is for your life. God has two kinds of desires. One is for the body as a whole, and the second is a unique goal for each individual.

### God's Corporate Will

God's corporate will is twofold: (1) for all to be saved and (2) for His children to live holy lives.

#### The Will for All to Be Saved

John 3:16–17 says, *"For God so loved the world that He gave His only begotten Son, that whoever believes in Him should not perish but have everlasting life. For God did not send His Son into the world to condemn the world, but that the world through Him might be saved."* And 1 Timothy 2:3–4 says, *"For this is good and acceptable in the sight of God our Savior, who desires all men to be saved and to come to the knowledge of the truth."* God doesn't want any of His children to perish. He desires greatly that we *all* be saved.

The moment you received Jesus Christ as your Lord and Savior, your "navigation system" was "installed" into your "car." Once you have received the Holy Spirit, you will be fully equipped for the ride ahead. This is the foundation on which our life purpose is built. We get from point A to point B by using what is inside of us.

If you are not fully equipped, but would like to be, turn to the appendix for your "installation instructions" (a simple prayer for salvation).

<u>The Will for All to Live a Pleasing and Holy Life</u>

It is God's will that His children live lives that are pleasing and acceptable to Him. Romans 12:2 NIV says, *"Do not conform to the pattern of this world, but be transformed by the renewing of your mind. Then you will be able to test and approve what God's will is—his good, pleasing and perfect will."* This verse has two parts to it. In order to get part two, you must do part one.

First, you need to have your mind renewed so that you don't keep doing the things the world expects you to do. After that's done, you'll be able to know what God's will is for your life. Those who are worldly-minded cannot understand the things that are spiritual. We must exchange our "flesh card" for our "spirit card" so we can understand the things of the Spirit, which encompasses our purpose.

In order to live a God-pleasing life, we need to know God's will. And in order to know God's will, we must be transformed by the renewing of our minds. After changing our mind-sets, we will be able to change our behaviors from being unholy to being holy, which is part of God's will for our lives.

*It is God's will that you should be sanctified: that you should avoid sexual immorality; that each of you should learn to control his own body in a way that is holy and honorable, not in passionate lust like the pagans, who do not know God; and that in this matter no one should wrong or take advantage of a brother or sister. The Lord will punish all those who commit such sins, as we told you and warned you before. For God did not call us to be impure, but to live a holy life. Therefore, anyone who rejects this instruction does not reject a human being but God, the very God who gives you his Holy Spirit. (1 Thessalonians 4:3–8 NIV)*
*God's Unique Will for You*

Once we have a clear understanding of God's will for the body, we can move forward to understanding what God has created us specifically to do. I believe there is a particular problem on this earth that God created *you* to solve!

Trying to accomplish your unique purpose in life without first understanding God's principal will for all of our lives is like going to a car dealership and picking out the color of the car, the interior, and a few special features and then telling the salesperson you want all of that but you don't want the engine.

The life of the car is in the engine. It is not in the fancy leather seats, the OnStar service, the wood-grain dashboard, or the twenty-two-inch chrome rims. All of these special features are lovely and have their purpose. But without the engine, nothing else matters. You may look great sitting in that car, but it won't get you anywhere.

Your unique purpose on earth is like all those special features. Jesus Christ, along with the Holy Spirit, is the engine that enables everything else to make sense.

-----------------

Some people mistakenly believe that everything that happens must be God's will. But certain individuals can speak things into existence that are not God's will. Scripture says that "death and life are in the power of the tongue" [16] and "the gifts and the calling of God are irrevocable."[17] Things spoken by people who have great authority in the spiritual realm carry much weight.

The use of prophecy is a great example of this. In 2 Kings 2:23–24, we read that the prophet Elisha cursed forty-two boys and had them killed. Was it God's will for those young men to be murdered? I am not convinced that it was. Yet it happened because it was the prophet's will.

Whatever the enemy uses for bad, however, God can turn around and use for good.[18]

There are three subcategories that fall under God's will for your life:

**God's perfect will.** This is God's ultimate goal and desire for your life, His perfect and spotless will.

To illustrate this concept, let's say that God's perfect will was for you to take two steps forward, move four steps to the left, hop forward twice, and then press a red button. If you did that, you would fulfill His perfect will for you.

**God's permissive will.** God allows some things to happen in order to allow us to see His sovereignty. Factoring in our foolishness, God permits us to experience the consequences of our poor decisions. Yet His grace and mercy enable us to receive His blessings, even though they may come with added pain and unnecessary suffering that we inflict on ourselves due to disobedience.

Jonah is a great example of this.[22] He went in the opposite direction of where God told Him to go, and he suffered a great deal because of his disobedience. Yet God gave him a second chance.

To use the illustration above, let's say that God tells you to take two steps forward, move four steps to the left, hop forward twice, and then press a red button. But after you take those first two steps forward, you move five steps to the left ... and you fall into a pit because you went too far. God gets you out of the pit, but you suffered a broken leg. So you take two hops forward, painfully, before you press the red button and get your prize.

**Our free will.** God does not interfere with our freedom to make our own choices. We can choose to completely disobey and disregard everything that He tells us.

Walking in our free will is like taking two steps backwards, moving four steps to the right, skipping forward four times, and missing the mark because we did not follow the instructions that He gave. You can't expect to walk in disobedience and receive all that He has promised for you.

------------------

We have all been in need of answers and guidance at some point in our lives. *What is my purpose? What is God's will for my life? What am I supposed to be doing in this season? When are things going to change?* These are all common questions. But gaining wisdom and responding to insight will propel you forward to that place of understanding, peace, and total fulfillment. Living to our fullest potential comes when we take what we know and apply it to our daily lives.

In the passage below, Luke tells us that the more we know, the more we will be held accountable for what we know. With an increase in insight comes an increase in responsibility. If you want God to share more revelation with you so you can walk 100 percent in His will, you will be held to a higher standard than those who have not been entrusted with as much revelation as you.

*That servant who knows his master's will and does not get ready or does not do what his master wants will be beaten with many blows. But the one who does not know and does things deserving punishment will be beaten with few blows. From everyone who has been given much, much will be demanded; and from the one who has been entrusted with much, much more will be asked. (Luke 12:47–48 NIV)*

## RECEIVE SIGNAL FROM THE SATELLITES
## ABOUT YOUR LOCATION

Not only does God want to talk to you about the overall purpose of your life, but He also wants to talk to you about your today. Before you can get into position, you first have to acknowledge that you are out of position. Essentially this is your Point A; where you currently are. There are several ways in which you can identify your Point A and the areas you are out of position.

*Someone Points it Out to You*

In football, a team can be penalized if there are too many players on the field at one time. When this occurs, the referee throws out a yellow flag. The team loses any yardage they may have gained on the play, and they have to redo the play if the ref didn't catch the infraction before the ball was hiked.

Being out of position not only slows our forward progress, it steadily pushes us further back from where we need to be. The way I see this is that there will come times in our life when we will make steady progression as we grow in Christ but at times we may lose focus. As a result we delay the forward progress we were making. Whenever we find ourselves operating out of God's will (His "rule book") we risk being moved out of position.

In order for a football play to be successful, everyone on the team needs to play his part and be in the right position. The quarterback has to stand right behind the center to receive the ball. The offensive linemen (left and right guards and tackles) need to get the blocks. The wide receiver needs to run the right route so the quarterback can get the ball to him. If the receiver does not get to the area of the field that the quarterback expects him to be in, he risks causing an interception or an incomplete pass.

If we are not in the area God has instructed us to be in, we run the risk of missing out when He comes, or even surrendering our blessing or destiny to someone else.

Every player on a football team needs to know what the route is going to be. If only the quarterback knew, how would the wide receiver know to split left or run a reverse? If only the receiver knew, how would the other offensive linemen know where to provide the blocks?

This is where accountability comes in. It is vital to have others on your team who know where you need to be so that when you get out of line they can correct you in love and help you during your spiritual warfare. True friends will pull the penalty flag when they notice something out of order. Proverbs 27:5–6 says (NIV), "Better is open rebuke than hidden love. Wounds from a friend can be trusted, but an enemy multiplies kisses".

As much as we hate having the whistle blown on us, it is important to have trusting friends put us back in line and keep us on track. Think about it. If you're doing something that is hurting you or someone else, would you rather have someone tell you you're okay or confront and correct you? Do you prefer sugarcoated feedback and diluted truths? Or do you want friends who speak the truth even if they step on your toes?

### You See it for Yourself

I started playing volleyball when I was in middle school and continued to play throughout high school. I didn't care much about passing, but I loved being on the front row so I could get the opportunity to spike the ball over the net. Playing the back row wasn't my strong suit, and the coach must have known that, because she normally subbed me out when it was time for me to rotate to the back.

But during one game in an area tournament, she did not sub me out. I was nervous because I didn't want to do anything to risk the win for us. The team we were playing had some girls who could hit hard! And guess where most of those hard balls landed? Yep, right in the back row.

During a time-out, the coach gave us a few pointers and encouraged us to keep fighting. Then we went back onto the court. The opposing team had the ball, and right away, Ms. Power Arm jumped up and slammed the ball so hard I couldn't return it.

Then I remembered what the coach had said during practice about aligning ourselves with the hitter so we could get a good pass. So I lined up my body in the direction that the hitter's arm was swinging. I stuck out my arms, ready to embrace the blow I was about to receive. I must have closed my eyes when she hit the ball, because I don't remember seeing myself pass the ball. But somehow I managed to land a nice pass to my setter.

We ended up winning that game and becoming the area champs (not only because of my wonderful passing, of course!). But I learned an important lesson from that experience. No matter how tough the opponent seems, if I get myself into the right position and do what I'm supposed to do, the game won't be as difficult and intimidating.

There is nothing the enemy can throw at us that we can't return to him. If we are in position, and following God's will, those attacks will not be as frightening as when we are out of position and getting blasted with one miserable circumstance after another.

Getting into position requires some self-evaluation. At times we may need someone to point it out to us, but we often already know. We all like to think that what we're doing is right but a lack of self-confrontation can be detrimental to our destiny. Denial is a defense mechanism that only hurts you.

Galatians 6:7 says that we reap the things we sow. If you plant oranges, don't expect to harvest apples. If you are out of position, don't expect God to give you profound revelations. If your mentality is "my way or no way," you won't reach your full potential.

So schedule a meeting with yourself. Sit down with God and ask Him to help you figure out what you're doing that's causing you to miss the mark with Christ.

*Pain Forces You to See It*

Our bodies are wired in such a way that they send pain signals to our brains to warn us when something isn't right.

If it weren't for pain, how would we know something was wrong? Although pain hurts, it is for our good.

Sometimes God uses emotional pain to get our attention to an area of our lives that needs to be fixed.

I have experienced a lot of pain in my personal relationships. I've gotten involved with guys who ended up hurting me. I cried and wailed and prayed and then cried some more. But when I look back on those times now, I realize the pain was for my good. It came during times when I was moving away from the will of God. My Christian walk had begun to sway and my focus became blurry. I wasn't seeing clearly and I certainly wasn't thinking clearly. I needed that pain because it got my attention back to where it needed to be: on Christ.

Pain helps us regain our focus and get back on track. So do not despise your pain. Open your heart and ask God to reveal to you the things in your life that are not right. If you already know some areas of your life that need adjusting, ask the Lord to help you get it together.

I've received a BA in psychology, A MS in professional counseling, and A PhD in clinical counseling. And I've had the concept of "operant conditioning" instilled in my memory from course to course. Operant conditioning is a type of learning in which behaviors are influenced mainly by the consequence that follow them.[23]

B. F. Skinner, a well-known behaviorist, created what is called an "operant conditioning chamber" (aka a Skinner box). As an experiment, Skinner put a rat into a box with a lever. Each time the rat pushed down on the lever with enough force, food was dispensed. After several attempts, the rat became conditioned to push the lever whenever he desired a reward of food. Skinner then decided to switch things up. Now, when the rat pushed the lever, instead of receiving food, it would get a small electric shock. The rat soon learned not to press the lever.

If you're like me, you've been in a "Skinner box" a time or two in your life. You found the person you thought was the perfect match for you. Your first few months together were pure paradise. He catered to you, she was all that plus a bag of chips, and everything was great. Every time you pushed that "lever of love," positive reinforcements came out. But after a couple of months, something changed. They aren't your normal sugar lumps anymore, more like a lump of coal. This person of your dreams stopped returning your phone calls. He or she is too busy to hang out with you on the weekends. You no longer receive heartwarming comments about how beautiful/handsome you are. You keep pressing that "lever of love," hoping to get back the old feelings, but nothing happens. You grow tired of getting "shocked" by the one who supposedly loves you. So what do you do? You stop pressing the lever. Because you realize that the more you press, the more negative consequences you get.

------------------

Dating relationships aren't the only tie-in to the "pain as a signal to change" concept. My brother bought me some roller skates several years ago. Wanting to at least look like I could skate, I went to YouTube and found some skating videos. I learned a couple of tricks and practiced them in my kitchen and bathroom before I went to the rink.

Unfortunately, I didn't practice enough, because when I got out there, I fell repeatedly. A girl skated up to me and said, "Mind if I give you some pointers?" Considering how many times I'd fallen, I wasn't about to turn down her offer. She told me the reason I couldn't do the trick I was attempting was that I wasn't positioning my feet correctly.

As I practiced the proper way, I felt a sharp pain in my right thigh. I told my new friend about it, and she pointed out that I was still not positioning my feet correctly. I tried to correct the problem, but wasn't sure what I was doing wrong. Finally, someone else approached me. She said she'd been observing me. Then she helped me position my legs correctly. Not only did I manage to perform the trick; I no longer felt any pain.

When we're hurting we feel the pain but we often don't understand why. But the Holy Spirit can inform us through a friend, a sermon, a dream, an answered prayer, or by some other means, what we're doing (or not doing) that is causing the pain. Pain forces us to step back and evaluate our lives. It opens our eyes to see that most of the pain we are going through is self-inflicted.

As I look back on many of my relationships, I can see that some of my hurts were caused by me! A guy would start off treating me right, but when that stopped happening, I kept hoping he would go back to the way things used to be. Too often we get into bad relationships, thinking, *I can help him/her change for the better. He/she just needs a little time.* But there is only one Savior, and it's not us. We need to stop pressing the lever, let the relationship go, and get ourselves back into position so God can romance us and reveal to us what true love is.

*Having a Lack of Peace*

A friend of mine attended the same master's program I did. One day he opened up and discussed with me the dissatisfaction he felt in his life. Although he was pursuing a degree, he was uncertain what he wanted to do with his life and what direction he was heading.

I could relate to his situation, because I'd felt that way during my undergraduate studies. After majoring in biology for three years, I asked myself one day, "What am I going to do with my life? Is this really the major I'm supposed to pursue?" I felt no peace about what I was doing and no passion about school.

So I stopped what I was doing and turned to God for answers about my direction in life. The Holy Spirit responded. He told me clearly that I was unsatisfied with what I was studying because that was not my purpose in life.

I was reluctant to switch to a different major because I feared I would have to study several more years to make up for lost time. But I finally made an appointment with my advisor, expressed my concerns and desires, and discussed what I needed to do to make the change.

God was surely in the mix of all this. Shortly after I switched, I found out that I wouldn't have to stay in school longer after all. As a matter of fact, I would get out earlier!

Many times fear likes to present itself as something real. I had no evidence that I would have to stay in school longer if I changed my major. My assumptions created fear over something that never really existed.

As soon as I switched my major, I had peace of mind about the decision. I began to enjoy going to class, and I felt confident in the direction I was going.

So when my friend expressed frustrations similar to the ones I'd experienced, I asked him if he'd prayed about what degree he should pursue. He admitted that he'd made the decision without consulting God first. I encouraged him to seek God's will about his career.

Philippians 4:6-7 tells us to "be anxious for nothing, but in everything by prayer and supplication … and the peace of God, which surpasses all understanding, will guard your hearts and minds through Christ Jesus." And Isaiah 26:3 tells us, "He will keep in perfect peace him whose mind is stayed on Him, because he trusts in Him."

If Christ is the center of everything we are doing, we should have peace in those areas. Now, that doesn't mean everything will happen exactly the way we want. But if you recognize the process God is taking you through, you can be content knowing that "He will complete the good work that He has started in you."[24] You may not be where you want to be yet, but you can know that you are on the right path to getting there.

If there are some areas in your life that you are a little shaky about, and your spirit isn't quite settled with them, evaluate those things and ask the Holy Spirit to reveal to you what it is that's making you uneasy. A lack of peace is usually a red flag, warning you that someone or something is out of position in your life.

*Rootless and Fruitless*

The purpose of a tree's roots is to supply it with nutrients and water so it can perform the functions it was made to do. Roots are also useful as an anchor for the tree, so it can remain stable. If a tree's roots are not properly grounded, it cannot receive what it needs to survive and thus will not bear fruit.

If you find yourself jumping from job to job, person to person, state to state, that instability may be a sign that you're out of position. Try doing a root check. How deep are you in the Word? You are a mighty oak tree (according to Isaiah 61:3 NIV), so surface roots just won't do!

Where there is no root you will not see fruit. If the work you do for the Lord has yet to yield any good fruit that may indicate that you are out of order somewhere in

67

your life. You wouldn't put money into a machine that had an "out of order" sign on it. So why should God continue to invest in us if we are not producing anything desirable and glorifying to Him? When we are bearing much fruit it brings God glory.

If you are not producing much (or any) fruit, perhaps you lack the nutrients needed to reproduce. To make you more fruitful, some fertilizer may have to be added to your life. A little "dung" never hurt anybody! It may look bad and smell awful, but it will make *you* look better when all is said and done.

## WHAT SEASON ARE YOU?

Knowing what season you are in will also help you to better pinpoint where you are. "There is a time for everything, and a season for every activity under Heaven" (Ecclesiastes 3:1 NIV). Environmentally, we have four seasons: winter, spring, summer, and fall. Each natural season brings about changes, with new experiences and opportunities. The same is true of our spiritual seasons. Every time we come out of a season, we should have a new nugget of understanding and wisdom we didn't have before.

Let's evaluate each season of life.

### Winter

The winter seasons in our lives are those times when it seems that we are waiting in isolation. We may feel that we are making minimal progress during this time.

I've had a number of winter seasons. They usually happen when I've been slowly drifting away from God. I may not have actually backslidden, but I've been focusing on my own agenda, and spending time with God became part of my "to-do list" ... hoping I could squeeze Him in before the day was over. Whenever I tried to put God on the back burner, He immediately tossed me into a wintery season.

I wouldn't call this a punishment, but more like a time of *recalibration.*

If you have one of those touch-screen cell phones, you know what happens when you tap your screen and keep missing the mark that you are trying to touch. When this happens you can go to your Settings to recalibrate your phone. Then you'll be able to hit the correct mark every time.

When we fall short of what God expects of us, we are missing the mark. So God has to help us re-prioritize and adjust some things in our lives.

Winter seasons can seem lonely and a bit irritating. But the most intimate times with a loved one are when the two of you are alone, with minimal distractions. That is what God wants: to get us alone, and to wrap us in His warm embrace. Some dead things needed to be removed from us so that we would have enough room to receive the new things He wants to reveal to us in our spring season.

*See! The winter is past;*
*the rains are over and gone.*
*Flowers appear on the earth;*
*the season of singing has come,*
*the cooing of doves*
*is heard in our land.*
*The fig tree forms its early fruit;*
*the blossoming vines spread their fragrance.*
*Arise, come, my darling;*
*my beautiful one, come with me.*
*Song of Songs 2:11–13 (NIV)*

## Spring

After a cold and dreary winter, nothing beats that wonderful feeling of a hot sun and a cool breeze touching your skin. At the slightest sign of an increase in temperature, flip-flops, shorts, and short-sleeved shirts are pulled from the bottom of the drawers so we can indulge in every sunny moment.

Springtime is symbolic of new beginnings. It represents freshness and the birth of new things. Things that disappeared in winter (like flowers and green grass) return. And things that were useless in the previous season (like gardening tools) are used abundantly in this one.

Spring is the time for discovery. Many opportunities, dreams, and visions can be planted inside you, and hopes can turn into reality.

In this season, I am full of creativity and innovative ideas. I'm constantly at my "drawing board," trying new things I can get my hands into and figuring out how I can obtain them.

This season is a time of refreshing freedom, where you can let your hair down. But it's not just a time of great leisure. In many areas of the country, spring is a time for planting, preparation, and intentionality.

Spiritually speaking, spring is a sowing season. This is the time to put forth your best efforts. Get down on all fours and do the nitty-gritty work. Praying without ceasing is important in any season, but during this time you want to be especially diligent and consistent in the time you spend with God as you position and prepare yourself to receive from Him.

In this season, don't wait for things to happen. Make them happen. If you want corn when harvest time comes, you'd better plant corn and prepare for it to come. If you want God to do something in your life, you'd better be praying, fasting, and diligently obeying all that He instructs you to do. When, where, and how you sow your time, money, and energy should be very strategic during this time of your life.

## Summer

Summertime is the season to kick back, relax, and sip lemonade. After working hard during the spring, you want nothing more than a great vacation. Summer is when schools are closed and families and friends gather together. Everything is at its fullest bloom and brightest color.

Spiritually, this is also a time for leisure and relaxation. You're not stressing to meet deadlines. You're as cool as cool can be.

As I stated earlier, I was in a season of rest for about six months. It was during the time between graduating with my master's degree and starting my doctoral program. At first relaxing was difficult for me. I had just finished my "spring" season, and I was accustomed to always doing something. Setting everything aside and just relaxing was hard because I felt like I was wasting time.

I wasn't, however. I was doing exactly what God wanted me to do ... which was nothing! I didn't work, I didn't read many books, I didn't attend any spiritually enriching training classes at church, I didn't get involved in extracurricular activities and God was perfectly okay with that. During this time He wanted me to focus on soaking in His presence day in and day out.

Since I was used to always producing something or making something happen, this season felt like a delay for me. I wasn't seeing anything new happen. Physically, my life stayed the same. That was tough at first. But I soon got the hang of it and became okay with doing nothing but sitting with God and getting to know Him and myself more. And it was by far the best season of my life.

I also discovered that a resting season was vital after my long and hard planting season, because I would need all the stored-up energy I could get to reap the abundant harvest that came next!

Fall

After you've worked hard, and then rested, it's time to reap. You've finally reached your harvest season. Everything you sowed will now be returned to you—and then some.

Galatians 6:7–9 (KJV) clearly explains the sowing and reaping process:

*Be not deceived; God is not mocked: for whatsoever a man soweth, that shall he also reap. For he that soweth to his flesh shall of the flesh reap corruption; but he that soweth to the Spirit shall of the Spirit reap life everlasting. And let us not be weary in well doing: for in due season we shall reap, if we faint not.*

Whatever you sowed during your planting season you will see in abundance during your reaping season. Remember that one small seed produces a multiplied harvest. God takes our 10 percent tithe and turns it into a blessing that is pressed down, shaken together, and running over (Luke 6:38). Isn't it amazing how He can use our little and make it something huge?

During this time, change will come to you and your surroundings. You do not act the same way you did before, and those who are close to you will either accept it or reject it. If they reject your positive change, they are like dead leaves that were going to fall away anyway, so let them go. If some stay, they may be a sturdy branch or root that will be with you regardless of the season, whether or not you have something to give. Those are the people you hold on tight to.

## YOU CAN'T DO IT ON YOUR OWN

*Go Home*

Okay. Now you know what season you are in, you have clearly identified your Point A, and you've realized that you may be out of position in some areas of your life. So what do you do next?

"Work on getting myself right so God can use me?" That sounds like a plausible answer, doesn't it? But it's incorrect. You will never be able to get yourself in order if you're depending on your own strength. What's the point of having a Savior if we could save ourselves? God knew we couldn't do it on our own, so He stepped in and bore the punishment for our sins.

The best step you can take after realizing that you are out of position is to go back home. "You mean move back into my parents' house?" No. Get yourself to that place where Jesus is. Wrap yourself in His arms of love and covering. If you've run away from home, return to your rightful place as the son or daughter of the living King. Make the commitment today to rededicate your life to Christ, or make the decision to come to Christ for the first time.[19]

The most beautiful story of restoration is the parable of the lost son in Luke 15:11–24. In this story, a young man was so focused on the world that his life became a complete mess. When he realized it, he decided to go back home. His father saw him from a distance, leaped for joy, and ran to cover his son with his best robe. The son had prepared a speech about what he had done wrong and how unworthy he was. But the father ignored it. Basically, he said, "You are my son regardless of what you've done. I'm just happy that you finally realized this is where you need to be. I am so glad to welcome you back home!" I love that the father didn't wait till his son stepped on the porch to greet him. He ran out to welcome him!

Maybe you've been super independent, wanting to do things your way. But you're ready to turn your back on the things of the world. Don't worry about taking a shower, brushing your hair and teeth, and buying new clothes and shoes before you return home. God will meet you right where you are, with open arms. Stop trying to fix yourself, because that's a waste of time. Clay doesn't tell the potter to leave it alone because it can make itself into a beautiful vase. Well, stop trying to shape your life without the help of your awesome Creator!

If you're struggling with addictions, give them to Him. If you're involved in difficult relationships, give them to Him. If finances are tight, give them to Him. If you're trying to stop any kind of sinful behavior, give it to Him.

You may be thinking, *But you don't know all the bad things I've done.* But in this parable, the father never once asked his son what he'd done while he was away from home or what he did with all of his money. So stop making excuses! God washes away all our sins when we repent and turn from our wicked ways.[20]

A navigation system can track your current location, no matter where you are, and get you to the destination you need to reach. How miserable would it be if your device made you go to a certain place before it could get you where you wanted to be? Could you imagine being on vacation in Arizona and wanting to go somewhere ten minutes away, but because you bought that GPS in Alabama, it assumed that was your starting point?

Oh, how lovely is the Holy Spirit's tracking device. He meets us right where we are. And despite how far off track we may have gotten, He is still capable of getting us into proper position.

*Let Go and Let God*

One of my best friends from college gave me a great example of what it looks like to try to hold on to what we want and also try to accept what God wants us to have at the same time. Imagine having something in your hand and gripping it against your palm with just your pinky and ring fingers; your thumb, index finger, and middle finger are still straight. Now imagine God wanting to give you a large cup to fill with blessings. But you can't accept it because half of your hand is occupied with something else. We can't take on God's agenda if our lives are so full of activities that only satisfy our carnal desires.

Breathing is another great example. You can't take in what you need (oxygen) until you release what you don't need (carbon dioxide). Exhale the things that are harmful to you, and then you'll be able to inhale all that is good for you. If you never breathe out, you can't breathe in, and eventually you'll pass out. So ask yourself this: is that person or thing you're holding on to worth losing consciousness for?

# STAY P.L.U.G.ged IN

A navigation system cannot run without power. When the battery starts getting low, a warning pops up on the screen, informing you of how much juice is left. If you don't plug into a power source soon, your device will no longer be of any use to you.

For believers, our power comes from constant communication with God through prayer, listening to and studying His Word, fellowshipping with other believers for support and accountability, and giving up those things that feed the flesh by way of fasting.

The Bible has a lot to say on these subjects. Here are a few examples.

*Praying*

- "Pray without ceasing." (1 Thessalonians 5:17)
- "The effective, fervent prayer of a righteous man avails much." (James 5:16)
- "The eyes of the Lord are on the righteous, and His ears are open to their cry." (Psalm 34:15)
- "Be anxious for nothing, but in everything by prayer and supplication …" (Philippians 4:6)
- "This kind [of demon] can come out by nothing but prayer and fasting." (Mark 9:29)
-

*Listening to and Studying God's Word*

- "Faith comes by hearing, and hearing by the word of God." (Romans 10:17)
- "Hear instruction and be wise, and do not disdain it. Blessed is the man who listens to me." (Proverbs 8:33–34)

- "My son, give attention to my words; incline your ear to my sayings." (Proverbs 4:20)
- "He who has ears to hear, let him hear." (Matthew 11:15)

*Uniting with Other Believers*

- "Two are better than one, because they have a good reward for their labor. For if they fall, one will lift up his companion. But woe to him who is alone when he falls, for he has no one to help him up." (Ecclesiastes 4:9–10)
- "… that you and I may be mutually encouraged by each other's faith." (Romans 1:12 NIV)
- "Where two or three are gathered together in My name, I am there in the midst of them." (Matthew 18:20)
- "My goal is that they be encouraged in heart and united in love, so that they may have the full riches of complete understanding, in order that they may know the mystery of God, namely, Christ, in whom are hidden all the treasures of wisdom and knowledge." (Colossians 2:2–3)
- "Bad company corrupts good character." (1 Corinthians 15:33 NIV)

*Giving Up Certain Foods*

- "When you fast, do not be like the hypocrites." (Matthew 6:16–18)
- "Turn to me with all your heart, with fasting, with weeping, and with mourning." (Joel 2:12–13)
- "Is this not the fast that I have chosen: to loose the bonds of wickedness, to undo the heavy

burdens, to let the oppressed go free, and that you break every yoke?" (Isaiah 58:6)

- In Scripture, fasting precedes major assignments and/or revelations. (See Exodus 24:18; 34:28; Deuteronomy 9:9, 18, 25–29; 10:10; Daniel 10:3-13; Matthew 4:2.)

## HOW TO KNOW IF YOUR BATTERY IS LOW

Mental-health service providers typically diagnose patients within the first few counseling sessions to come up with a treatment plan. The criterion for each issue or disorder is a list of symptoms that a person who had that diagnosis would exhibit.

I have created my own list of "symptoms" to help you determine if you qualify for a "disorder" I call "911.1 Low Battery Syndrome." See figure on the following page.

If any of these criteria fit you, you need to get plugged in to a power source so you can begin a treatment process toward restoration.

Mental-health service providers believe that the best plans are the ones clients create, because they are more likely to follow something they thought of themselves. I would like to make a few suggestions as you come up with your personal restoration plan.

First, make up your mind to implement the necessary changes. An unsteady mind will yield unsteady results.

Second, find a support team. You cannot do this on your own, because as you go through treatment, you may experience some withdrawal symptoms and temptations to relapse. Your flesh will not want to stop doing the things it loves, so you will need accountability.

## Mental and Emotional Health Corner
## 911.1 Low Battery Syndrome

A. The main symptom of this condition is a pattern of disobedience, rebellion, lack of initiative, and/or decline in several spiritual areas, during which one (or more) of the following are present:
1. Decreased appetite for hearing and/or reading the Word
2. Avoids positive social contact and/or seeking corruptible and compromising relationships
3. Reduced pain as a result of sinning and/or an increased desire for the things of the world
4. Feelings of disconnect from the Father
5. Distractibility; declined attentiveness to Christ
6. Reluctance to seek God's face and will for one's life
7. Lack of contentment with Jesus alone
8. Decline in patience
9. Wavering faith
10. Decrease in desire to please God and do His will
11. Loss of hope, feelings of guilt, doubtfulness, and/or shame
12. Contentment with being idle
13. Lack of peace
14. Suicidal ideation and/or attempts
15. Numb/apathetic
16. Easily irritated/often angry
B. The above-described disturbances in behavior cause spiritually significant impairment, which is reflected in personal as well as social functioning.
C. This condition can be:
   a. *Acute* if symptoms are just beginning;
   b. *Chronic* if symptoms have gone on for some time

When people want to stop drinking, they don't hang around friends who go to the bar and invite them to join them every weekend. The same applies to you. Whatever you want to do more or less of, find someone who will help support you and honor the decisions you've made.

Finally, replace your irrational beliefs with rational ones. Visualize yourself being released from your struggles. Free yourself of the belief that you can't change or that delivery will be too difficult.

Rational Emotive Behavioral Therapy is based on the belief that if the therapist can get the client to change his thinking, his feelings and behaviors will be transformed as well. I agree with this concept, because the human mind has tremendous power.

But before you can access this power, you need to put yourself in position to receive it. If your navigational device is not within a certain distance from the outlet, there is no way it can plug in to the power source.

The Bible says, "Draw near to God and He will draw near to you."[21] If you are not close to God, you are not in position to receive His power. You will soon run out of life and be of no good to yourself or others.

When a technological device loses power, we say it died. Do not let yourself die spiritually because of your unwillingness to get into position to receive all that God the Provider has for you.

1. What's your Point A? Write down where you are mentally, emotionally, spiritually, relationally, and professionally.
2. If you are out of position with the Lord, what would it take to get yourself back into position?
3. "In his heart a man plans his course, but the Lord determines his steps," says Proverbs 16:9. What have you been trying to do your way rather than allowing God to have His way in your life?
4. Are there some things or people in your life that are preventing you from getting to the place God wants you to be? What or who are they, and how are they blocking you from getting into position?
5. Are you afraid to be in isolation? If so, what are some things you can do to overcome that fear?
6. Read Job 14:13. What are some benefits of being in isolation?
7. The Bible tells of many times when people were isolated before they were given a major assignment (Jesus and Moses, for example). Why do you think this isolation period was necessary? Do you see how this can correlate with your need for isolation? Explain.
8. What areas in your life are you not at peace with? What causes you uneasiness?
9. If you want God to trust you with more, your behavior and character must show Him that He can. How do you plan to prove to God that He can trust you with more?

# STEP FOUR

## IDENTIFY YOUR POINT B: WHERE DO YOU WANT TO GO?

### KEY IN THE DESIRED END POINT

Some people don't think emotional or spiritual journeys are legitimate. They need to see or touch something to feel they've reached a certain goal: a trophy, a certificate, a final grade, a relationship. However, we don't need anything physical to grasp to prove our fulfillment.

Truth to tell, these types of journeys aren't completely intangible. The fruit of our personal walk with Christ will be evident when you step into the world. The level of influence you'll have on the world will be dependent on the amount of time you spent in your secret place with God.

*Ask for Wisdom*

Letting the Holy Spirit take the lead in your journey is important, because He will point things out to you that you weren't even aware of. For example, once my gifting of dreams was stirred up, I began having multiple dreams every night. In one series of dreams, the Holy Spirit repeatedly tried to reveal to me that I needed inner healing. I wasn't sure what I needed healing for. I didn't have any memories of things in my past that I was still hurting from. I thought I was fine. I asked for clarification several times, but the Holy Spirit just kept telling me I needed healing.

Eventually He revealed to me areas hidden deep in my heart that had left me wounded. I'd forgotten about them, not seeing them as a big deal. But spiritually and emotionally, I had an open wound.

If I hadn't allowed the Holy Spirit to show me where I was wounded, I would still be dying a slow emotional and spiritual death because of my inability to see the core of my issues. I encourage you to ask the Holy Spirit if there are any areas in your life that you are unaware of that need inner healing. If so, take His hand and let Him walk you through them.

*Be Specific*

When you get in alignment with God's Word, His desires become your own. The things you want will be those things that He longs for you to have.

If you momentarily forget the good things He wants you to seek after, and you begin to veer down the wrong path, the Holy Spirit will snap you back to reality. "Hold up. Wait a minute. You're going the wrong way. In two blocks, make a U-turn and you'll be back on track."

Your Internal Navigation System is the greatest accountability partner you could ever have because He knows what's best for you. When someone or something tries to take you down the wrong road, the Holy Spirit won't say, "Hey, you missed your turn, but that's fine. You can hang out in this neighborhood for a while, and then I'll get you back on track." No way. Doing things that are wrong is bad for you. The Holy Spirit won't play around with your destiny. And neither should you.

You know what you want in life. If something comes along that doesn't meet the standards you've set, keep moving. Don't let it delay your progress. You entered your destination before you began the journey. So don't be tempted to take whatever is thrown at you along the way. Keep your vision focused. Don't let it be distorted by passing things that will try to capture your attention.

Nobody is perfect, so there will come a time when you get a bit off the path. That's understandable. Just make sure you quickly get back on the right track.

## HAVE A PLAN

If you want to get from point A to point B, you don't just hop in your car and enter some random address into your GPS and say, "Guess I'll go there today." No, you decide where you want to go and then find the address of that location.

God doesn't come up with random places to take you. He has strategically planned out exactly where He wants you to go. Jeremiah 29:11 (NIV) reminds us, "He knows the plans He has for us … plans to proper us and not to harm us, plans to give us hope and a future." Psalm 139: 16 (NIV) says, "All the days ordained for me were written in your book before one of them came to be." This journey you are on is not a game to God. His plan is to complete the good work that He started in you (Philippians 1:6).

## GET ON BOARD

*Heed the Instructions*

When I conducted group-counseling sessions with children, one of our rules was that when someone else was talking the rest needed to have quiet lips and listening ears. This elementary rule has spiritual applications. To set a conducive atmosphere for the Holy Spirit to speak to us about our destinations, we need to remove the distraction of self, shutting our mouths and opening our ears to what He has to say.

If two people are talking at the same time, they are talking *at* each other, not *to* each other. Both will miss part of what the other is saying. Effective communication involves listening and then responding accordingly.

I love watching *Family Feud*. Partly because Steve Harvey is so funny. But also because it takes great cognitive ability to quickly listen to the question and then respond immediately with an answer off the top of your head. I laugh when a family member hits the buzzer before the host finishes the question and then gives an answer they would not have said if they'd waited to hear the entire question. For example, on one show, Steve Harvey started with "What does a woman do for her baby—" The buzzer went off and a girl shouted, "Change his diaper!" The answer was not up there. With a smirk, Steve Harvey finished the question: "What does a woman do for her baby that she also does for her husband?" The woman who rushed to speak missed some vital information that would have helped her respond more appropriately.

We will find ourselves in that same predicament if we rush past the Holy Spirit and don't give Him a chance to impart the necessary things into our lives. We need to be attentive and fully engaged as we commune with the Father as He guides us. Listening is a key ingredient to reaching our destination.

Here is a prime example. When my brother told me that he and his friend were coming to visit me one weekend, I planned several fun activities for us to enjoy. One of them was going to a facility that had a game room, go-karts, a batting cage, and more. I called the place to get the address. The man who answered tried to give me detailed directions, but I didn't pay attention. I had the GPS and an address—I didn't need anything else.

When the three of us got together, we hopped in the car and I entered the address into my GPS. Thirty minutes later we pulled up to a deserted building. I called the place again. The man who answered told me I had the right address but the wrong zip code. The street we were on stretched across the city and into another one. The man told me to head toward Memphis instead of Clarksville, and that made all the difference.

As I thought back to when I first called, I realized that the man had tried to tell me specifically where the place was, but I tuned him out after he gave me the address. I heard only the part I wanted to hear because I believed my GPS would handle the rest. If I had listened to the full instructions, we would not have gotten lost or gone an hour out of our way.

We tend to think we can succeed by our own skills, wits, and assets. But these man-made resources are insufficient. We need every detail of the Holy Spirit's guidance and instruction in order to reach our desired destination. Leaning on our own understanding and having selective hearing will delay our process and get us far off track.

God does not waste words. When He speaks, He does so with a purpose. Listen to all that He has to say, even if you feel that some of the information is irrelevant or unimportant. If it doesn't have meaning in your life at the moment, it will down the road.

------------------

My car came with a built-in navigation system. I also have a store-bought one I can stick in my windshield. The built-in system gives me the option of adjusting two volumes: the navigator's voice and the radio. But no matter how high I turn up the radio volume, the navigator's voice always overpowers it when the system is in use. It doesn't get louder; it automatically turns down the radio volume when it is speaking.

Well, I love listening to music in my car, and having a voice constantly interrupting my songs got a little irritating. So one day I decided to turn the navigator's volume all the way down. When it started giving me instructions, I didn't hear the words, but I knew it was saying something because it paused my music.

The Holy Spirit is very persistent in doing whatever it takes to get our attention. If we try to ignore Him, He will put a pause on whatever we're enjoying that is causing us to ignore Him.

What pauses have you seen in your life? Perhaps the loss of a job you were spending more time on than you did with Him? Or an injury that caused you to "slow your roll"? Did spending some time in prison enable you to get your life straight? Maybe an unexpected pregnancy convinced you to set aside some risky behaviors. Have you had one too many unsatisfying and unhealthy romantic relationships? Or been separated from friends when you began to idolize them?

Before God has to intervene, think about the people and things in your life that do you no good. Then put your finger on the "pause" button and press.

*Trust His Guidance*

Wherever God plans to take us, He has the best of intentions. We can trust that He won't lead us astray.

I've never seen a baby ask adults for their credentials before allowing them to pick her up. Babies trust that you won't harm them.

Have you ever gone into the cockpit of a plane and asked the pilot how many years of flying experience he has so you can assess his competence? No. You trust that he knows what he's doing.

Why is it so easy to trust people with our food, shelter, safety, even our very lives, yet hard to trust the one who has made known His plan for us? The Lord says, "I know the plans I have for you. Plans to prosper you and not to harm you, plans to give you hope and a future."[25] Many other places in Scripture tell us how He guides, leads, and directs our every step to get us to our desired place. In Proverbs 3:5–6 we are told to "trust in the Lord with all your heart, and lean not on your own understanding; in all your ways to acknowledge Him, and He shall direct your paths." If we entrust our destiny to His hands, we are guaranteed guidance and counsel from Him.

A GPS can show you a satellite view of your entire route. This allows you to see your final destination before you get there. But it doesn't tell you about all the stuff you'll have to go through to get there. It doesn't show the waits you will encounter at stoplights. Or traffic delays or detours due to road construction. Nor does it tell you what the weather will be along the way. All it shows is your starting point and your ending point.

God shows us where we are, and He promises that where He plans to take us is good. But He doesn't give much insight into the details of the trip. If we knew how long we would have to wait in unexpected traffic jams or at stoplights, we'd probably never start the journey.

That's why He doesn't reveal to us every hurt, heartache, and pain we'll have to endure. He knows our minds cannot process all that, and we would forfeit our destiny without giving it a shot.

## IMPLEMENT THE PLAN AND GET MOVING

*Not Moving Hurts You More*

At a church event one year, I was responsible for coordinating all of the activities for the children. One of the games I decided to play was musical chairs. In this game, chairs are placed in a circle, backs facing inward. The number of chairs is one less than the number of participants. Everyone walks around the chairs while the music is playing, and when the music stops, the goal is to sit in a seat as fast as you can. The one person without a chair has to sit out. Rounds continue until there is one winner.

As I orchestrated this game at the church event, the little ones played a few rounds before I noticed a commotion around one of the chairs. I walked over to investigate and found a little girl about five years old balled up in the chair. I asked her what was wrong. "Nothing," she said. I asked why she wasn't moving around in a circle like everyone else. "If I don't stay here, I might lose!"

This little girl had the idea that if she remained stagnant, she would win because the point of the game was to get a chair. She wanted to take the easy way to victory and cut straight to the chase instead of going through the process like everyone else.

I tried to explain to her that she would never know the outcome of the game if she didn't get up and try. But she was still reluctant to play by the rules. I decided that it was only fair to sit her out while the others continued to play. Because she was disqualified, she still ended up losing. Her lack of effort and unwillingness to move cost her the game.

90

If a fear of moving, or fear of the unknown that lies ahead, is keeping you from venturing out, you will lose. God is progressive; He's always moving and doing. So if we remain still, there is no way we can stay with Him. If "faith is the substance of things hoped for and the evidence of things not seen,"[26] there will be times when the future is unknown to us. That's why we are told to lean not on our own understanding but to trust in Him.[27]

All of the miracles we read about in the Bible involved action from the people involved. The man with the withered hand had to stretch out his hand before it was healed (Matthew 12:13). The sick man at the pool of Bethsaida had to rise, take up his bed, and walk (John 5:8). The man born blind had to go wash in the pool of Siloam (John 9:7). The paralyzed man brought to Jesus had to arise, take up his bed, and go home (Matthew 9:6).

Others may be able to intercede on our behalf, but action is still required of us. The paralyzed man's friends knew Jesus could heal him, but they had to tear off the roof of someone's house to get him to Jesus.

If we want something, we have to put some pep behind our step to obtain it. God will do His part, but we must do our part as well.

In one of my graduate courses for counseling, we discussed the difference between helping people who aren't helping themselves versus helping people who are actually trying and just need an extra push of motivation. We all agreed that it is difficult to help someone who doesn't desire to make changes and take the steps. One student said she could sit in her closet all day and pray that God will give her a hotdog but if she doesn't get up and do what it takes to get that hotdog then she will not get one. God wants us to take the initiative. After all, faith without works is dead, right? Yes, God will provide, but what are we doing to show that we trust Him?

That place where Abraham was about to sacrifice his son wasn't called Jehovah Jireh ("the Lord will provide") until after he demonstrated his faith by going up the mountain as God directed him. After Abraham's act of obedience to the instructions he was given, God demonstrated His provision (Genesis 22:14).

The Lord blesses our active obedience.

*Your Progress Should Be Evident to Others*

I like to keep my vehicle squeaky clean at all times— shiny tires and all. One weekend, I took a road trip, and all kinds of bugs and bird excretions found the front of my truck. By the time I got home, Diamond (my car) was a disaster! I didn't have time to clean it up right away, so I drove to all of my meetings with a filthy car.

After a lunch meeting one of my associates asked if I'd driven out of town that weekend. "Yeah, I did," I said. "How did you know?" He told me he could tell because of the mess on my truck.

The evidence that you are making progress should be all over you for others to see. You won't have to say a word about the changes you've made to reach your destination. It will be noticeable. You'll look different, talk differently, walk differently, react differently, even smell different. When you are en route to your destiny, there is no way you can remain the same as when you were heading down the road of destruction.

The evidence of progression in your life will make people curious. They'll want to draw closer to you so they can see what you've been doing differently and where you're headed next. If nobody is asking you "Where have you been?" or "How do you do that?" or "What's next after this?" that may signify that you don't have any "bugs or bird excretions" on your life.

A parked vehicle doesn't get messy (unless it's parked under a tree but you're missing the point). It has to be in motion. The same goes for you. No one will ever know that you are moving unless you get out of your "comfort zone parking space," shift gears to "Drive," and follow the path God has laid out for you.

*Timing Is Based on Your Forward Movement*

<u>Time and Progress</u>

Once you enter a destination into your GPS, it will display the current time and your estimated time of arrival. This estimate can increase or decrease depending on your speed, unanticipated traffic, stoplights—anything that stalls your forward progress. Aside from the uncontrollable factors, you can determine whether you arrive on time or late.

Your movements control the device. When you are in motion, the number of miles decreases. The amount of time to your destination also decreases. The navigation voice constantly tells you when a shift in direction has to be made.

When you stop, the only change is that the clock continues ticking. Your lack of movement is wasting time, postponing your arrival at your destination. The longer you remain stagnant, the more you delay your anticipated time of arrival.

Many cry out, "Lord, why aren't You doing anything? Why aren't You blessing me or delivering me?" What they fail to realize is that their laziness, their unwillingness to change, and their refusal to take the first step are the reasons for their delayed breakthroughs and blessings. Don't blame God if you aren't where you think you should be. Ask yourself … are you moving or not?

### The Voice

The voice of a navigation system talks when there's a course change you'll need to make soon. It also talks while you're making those turns and adjustments. It does not talk to you, however, when you're not moving.

If you haven't started driving, what would be the point of telling you the second turn if you haven't even completed the first? How funny would it be if we entered an address into the GPS and the first thing it said was "Please start driving." We would laugh and say, "Duh," right?

Wisdom works the same way. He won't waste His breath telling you something you already know or something that is obvious.

I once heard a pastor say that people need to stop looking for God to send signs, words, or confirmations for things we already know He has told us to do. People often say, "Lord, when You show me something, then I'll move." But God is saying, "I'll show you something after you start moving."[28]

This word slapped me in the face, because I have been guilty on numerous occasions of feeling like I needed to know all the details before making a move. I was trying to be cautious about not making a mistake, but in reality I was not trusting the word God gave me.

Your navigation system will not give you instructions when you have miles to go before the next direction is needed. If you were several miles away from your exit, you wouldn't want your device to tell you about it, because you'd probably forget it. And when the exit came up, you'd miss it.

Don't worry if you're heading to your destiny and you can't hear God speaking to you. His apparent lack of communication is not necessarily an indication that something's wrong. It may just mean that you have a ways to go before He wants to show you the next step.

The Holy Spirit knows our limits and our shortcomings, and He only gives us what we can handle. If He knows we will forget or mishandle a certain piece of information, He will withhold it from us until we are ready. If you believe you are heading down the right path but aren't sure where to turn next, just keep going straight. When it's time for you to make a move, you will clearly hear His voice in plenty of time. He'll give you a heads-up when there are changes that need to be made.

The GPS doesn't wait until you are right up on your turn or exit to tell you about it. Neither does your Internal Navigator. The Holy Spirit gives us instructions in a timely manner that doesn't put our lives in danger.

Can you imagine being in the fast lane on the freeway and hearing the navigation device tell you to take the next exit just as you are about to fly past it? Getting over and off in time would be nearly impossible and very dangerous!

This is one way to discern whether the voice giving you instructions and directions is God. If something sounds dangerous or harmful to you or those around you, take heed.

The voice of the navigation system remains the same whether you are on track or not. If you get sidetracked or lost, it won't criticize you or call you stupid. It doesn't tell you you're getting on its nerves. In an even tone, it simply says, "Rerouting." If you get turned around it will calmly tell you to make the next U-turn. No matter what you do, it will keep guiding you until you get to where you need to be.

If I were trying to give someone instructions, but he or she kept missing the turns I gave, I'd undoubtedly end up raising my voice or copping an attitude. So when I get turned around or sidetracked, I half expect my navigation system to yell at me or at least heave a deep sigh over having to constantly repeat itself and reroute for me.

Scripture says that Jesus never raised His voice (Isaiah 42:2). Yes, there were times when He got upset or angry. But even in His times of frustration, He never lost His cool. I'm so grateful that the Holy Spirit's temperament is not like ours!

WHAT'S ENTERED INTO YOU?

You have a destination attached to your life. And your Internal Navigator will guide you there, no matter how off track you get. God has a set plan for you, and He will not switch destinations if you venture off course for a while.

How can you know if you get off track? You'll feel a gentle tug. A little pull that continues until you get back to where you need to be.

Sometimes I will enter a destination into my GPS, then decide to run a quick errand before I head there. I miss the first right turn it told me to take, so it tells me to make the next right turn. I miss that one too. So it tells me to make a U-turn. The navigator continues giving me instructions that I'm not interested in, and keeps interrupting the music I'm trying to listen to, which is really annoying. But it doesn't care. Its objective is to get me back on track. It won't stop until I adhere to its instructions.

Jeremiah said God is like fire shut up in his bones (Jeremiah 29:11 NIV). He just won't leave you alone. Since you can't ignore Him, you might as well stop trying.

I believe we each have an assignment here on earth—to solve a problem, fix something, change something, do something. In order for you to solve any problem, you first have to get into position and get into purpose.

Think about something in your life that really bothers you, that always rubs you the wrong way. (One thing that pricks my heart is seeing young girls without guidance in life, heading in the wrong direction.) Ask yourself, "What am I going to do about that?" The Holy Spirit has put that nudge in you for a reason. Step out today and respond to that direction and see where the road carries you.

## YOU ARE NOT ALONE ON THIS JOURNEY

One day, while on an airplane, I looked out the window as we were landing and noticed the shadow of the airplane "flying" through the trees. Psalm 91:1 came to mind: "He who dwells in the secret place of the Most High shall abide under the shadow of the Almighty." At that moment I received a new revelation for this verse. I'd always thought it meant we are to follow Christ. But that day on the airplane, I gained a fresh insight.

Shadows can go places and endure things that we typically could not. People who "abide under the shadow of the Almighty" can get through tough situations and obtain things that seem unreachable. Because accompanying us in His shadow are grace, mercy, and favor.

That's how you got through that horrific trial. That's how you landed that job even though you didn't meet the qualifications. That's how you were able to endure abuse as a child and stand strong today. Because you were resting in His shadow, you were able to walk through things that would've knocked you out if you attempted them in your own strength.

Shadows can appear in front of you, beside you, or behind you, depending on the time of day. There are times in your life when you can see the hand of God ahead of you as you follow in His steps. Other times, you will feel that you are alone on your journey, but you are still in His shadow because Christ will never leave you. He has just shifted from pulling you to your destination to pushing you toward it. Regardless of where He is positioned, you always have a Guider and Guarder all around you. As Isaiah 52:12 (NIV) reminds us, "You will not leave in haste or go in flight; for the Lord will go before you, the God of Israel will be your rear guard."

---

### The Mental and Emotional Health Corner
### WHEN LONELINESS AND FATIGUE STRIKE

If you are feeling lonely on this journey called life allow me to comfort you by saying that you are not alone! Many of us feel that we are all alone bearing the weight of what God has asked us to do. We may even have family and friends around but someone still feel lonely. The feeling you get may be a cry from your soul to be refilled. If you are anything like me, you are probably so use to always being on the go and pouring into others that you often neglect to slow down long enough to be poured into and refilled. When we find ourselves running on fumes we end

---

up at a place that I call *Journey Burnout*. It's that point we reach when we have gone as far as we can, doing what we have been doing. It's that point we get to when we are a few minutes away from throwing in the towel. It's that place we get to when we think, why in the world am I doing this?! Sadly, it's the place where many dreams and visions are aborted, not because you didn't want it, but because you didn't have the nutrients and substance to carry it full term. To avoid journey burnout you must know yourself, know your limits, and know your capacity. Don't wait until you are seconds away from quitting. Recognize the early warning signs and give yourself a "journey break" by resting, eating (literally and spiritually), and by going back to the drawing board to be sure your energy and effort match the impact you desire to see.

⊹ *Food For Thought* ⊹

1. What is your Point B? Write down where you desire to be mentally, emotionally, spiritually, relationally, and professionally in the next 3 months, 1 year, 5 years, and 20 years.
2. Do you have actions to back up your professed faith in what God has spoken? What can you do to become more proactive in what you believe?
3. Why is it so important to be productive? How can you become more productive in your life?
4. In order to follow God's instructions, we need to know His voice. How does the Holy Spirit communicate with you (dreams, visions, audibly, feelings)?
5. Read 1 Kings 19:9–13. It is an example of the importance of being able to differentiate what is His voice and what is not. (If you are uncertain, ask God to speak to you more clearly and more often so you can fine-tune your spiritual ears).
6. Quieting your spirit is vital to hearing Him. So spend time "soaking" (intentionally resting) in His presence and meditating on His Word.
7. Have you ever resolved to settle for second best because you felt God's way was taking too long?
    a. What was the outcome of you settling?
    b. What strategies can you create for yourself to assure that you do not fall back into a settling state?

# STEP FIVE

## PREPARE FOR THE STUFF IN BETWEEN POINT A AND POINT B

### DON'T COMPARE YOURSELF OR YOUR JOURNEY WITH OTHERS

Imitation may be flattering, but it can lead you down a tumultuous road. In Psalm 139:14 it says that we were all "fearfully and wonderfully made." This doesn't mean that God's hands were shaking nervously as He was making us. In the Hebrew language, the word *fearfully* is *yare'* which means "standing in awe" when used of a person in an exalted position.[29] Wow! That means we are *awesome!*

*You Are Unique*

Can't you just picture God creating you? He's in His art room, with no distractions. He puts every strand of hair on your body with gentle care. He gently smoothens the clay with His hands and creates your head and your eyes and your toes. Every freckle He puts in just the right spot. Every dimension of every part of your body is thought out in great depth and with intricate detail. He puts in your extroverted or introverted tendencies and your love for animals, kids, or the elderly. And after God puts on the last finishing touches and polishes you up, He says, "You are good!"

You are not a mistake or an accident. So why would you even try to put on someone else's identity? If God needed two of someone, He would have made two. He made you just the way you are, because He knew that the things He would have you do and the people He would have you reach would need someone who looked liked you, talked

101

like you, acted like you, worked like you, and interacted like you.

Don't try to be an SUV if you're on a NASCAR track. And don't try to be a race car on a busy, pothole-filled city street. Your external and internal makings were not created for such environments. If God did not equip you for a certain life, a particular career, or a specific ministry, it will show eventually, because God's grace and anointing will not be upon you to do such a thing.

In *The Threshing Floor Revival,* Bishop T. D. Jakes said that being anointed is not about style; it's about power.[30] Trying to imitate someone's gestures, dress, dialect, etc. will not result in your having their anointing. Hone in on what you are designed to do. Then watch God move in your life.

*Different People, Different Routes*

There is more than one route to reach any location. And there is more than one way to obtain a particular goal or reach a certain mile marker in life. Two people may have similar destinations, but the journey that each has to travel to get to that point is unique. One might endure many roadblocks, delays, and frustrations, while the other has a pleasant travel with minimal bumps and stops along the way. Don't waste time and energy wishing you had what someone else has. You don't know what they had to go through to get there. If you want the end result, you have to take the process along with it. It's a package deal.

For people who are born into families with actors and actresses, getting into show biz is just a phone call away. Others have to endure many sleepless nights memorizing scripts for plays, trying to build their CVs, and standing in endless lines for casting calls. Some people are automatically recognized because of the clout their names hold in society, while others have to fight tooth and nail to

102

get recognition. In the same way, some pastors were the successor of a mega church, while other pastors started in a basement with a handful of faithful members and then worked their way up to thousands.

Everyone can benefit from a handout every once in a while. But the things we find most valuable and are most proud of are the things we had to work for and earn. In the movie *The Longest Yard,* the captain of the prison warden's football team complained about playing in a "fixed game" because the victory would have been phony.

The race Christ has placed us in is "fixed" in a sense because we already know we will win in the end. That's a game worth sticking out. Instead of seeking out the world's way of gaining success and doing anything and everything unrighteous or displeasing to God, we should strive for authentic success that will honor Him.

*Put in the Work*

How you get to your destination can determine whether you will stay there. God values a healthy work ethic. Many Scripture passages mention the importance of being diligent and intentional in all that we do. Why? I think it's because God knows that if we have to put our own efforts into something, we will have more appreciation, respect, and delight in it. I also believe God knows that giving us a working part in the process will strengthen us, and make us more knowledgeable and better equipped to handle and maintain what He has blessed us with.

If the owner of a multi-million-dollar company wanted to pass his business down to his eldest son, he would probably have the boy work under him for a few years first to assure that he was competent to run the place. If the father brought the son in with no experience, he'd be taking a huge risk of causing the business to deteriorate due to the new leader's incompetence.

Our Heavenly Father is the owner of the successes we are striving toward. But He knows we will be unfit unless He first takes us under His wing and trains us. Your ministry has God's name over it, and He is not about to let you make Him look bad. So He will prepare you before He hands the ministry over for you to steward.

If you have to climb your way up the ladder, you will develop many skills along the way. These skills, along with God's favor and provision, will help keep you there.

Today's generation wants to be "microwaved" to their destination without having to go through the process. *No process* and *reach destiny* in the same sentence will be an oxymoron to God. We have to be diligent and put in the work.

## TYPES OF ROUTES

Once you have the address entered into your GPS, the system shows you its suggested route. But it doesn't begin guiding you until you start following the path it has set before you … or you try an alternate route. You have to be active in the process.

The Holy Spirit is waiting for you to express an act of surrender, stating that you will obey His commands and follow His lead. He can't begin guiding you until you submit to His calling on your life. "Before us He has set life and death, blessings and cursing" (Deuteronomy 30:19). Everything we do requires a choice. Even the route you take is your choice, because God gives us a free will.

God instructed Jonah to travel to a specific location: Ninevah. Jonah did not like the request, because Ninevah was an uncomfortable place for him. He saw God's request as an inconvenience, and he wanted to avoid it So he decided to try to get away from God, not realizing that he could never hide from the Lord (Jonah 1-3).

Sometimes the Holy Spirit instructs us to do things we don't want to do. So we continue on our merry way, not realizing that the word God has set forth will come to pass one way or another. Scripture says in Isaiah 55:11 that God's word will never return to Him void. What He wants it to do will be accomplished. If He has to send a *whale-like* situation to swallow us up and get us to surrender, He will.

The convenience route is by no means free; it can cost you a great deal. How much have you invested in "ships" that you thought were going to carry you into wonderland, only to find that they led you into a storm? Relation*ships* that you gave your all to yet got nothing from except a crushed heart and spirit. Partner*ships* that you invested great amounts of time in before you got shortchanged and backstabbed. Friend*ships* where BFF turned out to stand for Big Fake Fony.

These "ships" may make you feel good for a time, but after a while you get seasick spiritually, mentally, physically, and emotionally. Don't let these "ships" take you down the convenience route, away from God's purpose for your life.

*The Alternative Route*

"All we like sheep have gone astray; we have turned every one, to his own way" (Isaiah 53:6). We, like sheep, have an innate tendency to veer off course, away from the group and from our Shepherd. We think we can mange on our own and make do under our own strength. However, we are unqualified to lead our own lives. If a sheep knew how to keep it together, there would be no need for a shepherd.

If you're on this alternative route, you may say to God, *I know You've set this particular route before me. But what I had in mind was a little bit different. So I'm going to follow the plan I worked out. It's sort of like Yours, because it will get me the same result, so in the end, I'll be good. So please bless me and the works of my hands. In Jesus' name. Amen.*

You may not have said this out loud, but your behavior shows it. You figure you'll give God a helping hand … as if He needed it. In your mind you have aggregated all of your desires, placed them on your agenda with an unambiguous timeline, turned on your timer, and shot the gun, expecting God to work under your authority and supervision.

Isaiah 45:9–11 (NIV) tells us that God knows what He is doing. Questioning Him and His works will not make matters better for us. He doesn't need us to tell Him when, where, how, and to what extent things need to be done. He runs His own watch. If he wants to flick the clock hands to go back in time, He can. And if He so pleases, He can turn the hands forward to go ahead of us. Placing your own demands on God does not make Him move any quicker.

We fall victim to wanting to create alternative routes when it doesn't feel like God is moving fast enough, or even moving at all. We want to hurry the process along. But then we begin to lose focus on God and no longer trust in His ability to provide for us.

Proverbs 14:12 says, "There is a way that seems right to a man, but its end is the way of death." Proverbs 16:25 says the same thing. Between these two passages are verses discussing wisdom, fools, sorrow, concerns of the heart, wickedness, evil, humbleness, fear of the Lord, and similar topics. These chapters also contain several contrasts, like "A fool despises his father's instruction, but he who receives correction is prudent" (Proverbs 15:5).

After God gives us our designed route, we will face many decisions that will determine whether we'll stay on the route we're given or if we'll try to find an alternative that we feel will better suit us. These decisions test our desire to be righteous, our faithfulness, our decision-making, our hearts, and our trust in and knowledge of the Lord.

After we've made a few of these great decisions, God gives us a friendly reminder of why we chose His path to follow in the first place. Along the way He gently urges us not to fall into the trap of becoming foolish and trusting in our "instincts" or "intuition."

-----------------

When I enrolled in the master's program at Lipscomb University, I chose the sixty-one-hour professional counseling track. One of the requirements was to take two practicums and one internship in the last three semesters. I began to look for my practicum site about nine months in advance. The first place I applied to was the one I really wanted to work at, but they told me they weren't sure they would receive the grant that would allow them to take on any new people. I didn't let that get me down. I continued in the application process—calling, e-mailing, and making interviews, hoping for a position. Nearly nine months passed, and I was getting discouraged. I had to have a site secured soon.

I started rationalizing what was going on and came to the conclusion that maybe God didn't want me to continue in the sixty-one-hour program. Perhaps He wanted me to switch to the thirty-six-hour program (which didn't require a practicum or internship). I struggled with this for a while and finally prayed about it.

One Sunday morning before church, I was asking God to make it clear to me what He wanted me to do. I was planning on changing tracks that week, and I wanted to be sure about that decision, because once I switched I wouldn't be able to change my mind again.

When the sermon started, I heard the message titled "Stay There." I could've left right then and there. I had already received my answer. But I didn't realize that until I got home and phoned a friend about my decision-making dilemma. When I told her what that morning's sermon title was, she said, "Trillion, that's your answer right there!" At that moment I knew God was showing me I needed to trust Him to get the right position for me, not rely on myself or my credentials.

The deadline passed for submitting contracts for our site, and I still didn't have one. The director, who was very understanding, gave me a little more time to secure a place. That very next week I received an e-mail from the first place I applied to, the one I really desired. The director asked if I was still looking for a practicum site. I leaped with joy at the realization of how God provided once I put my trust in Him. I went in for a second interview and was offered the position before I even walked out of the door!

In my eyes it made logical sense to switch programs when I couldn't secure a site. I assumed that all those closed doors, with none opening, constituted a sign for me to steer in a different direction. I almost made a big mistake based on my idea that taking the alternate route would better suit me in my situation.

God wanted me to go a certain route. But due to "hindrances," I felt the need to try a different way. His permissive will would have allowed me to get to the place He originally had in mind. However, I would have been on a path that may have included more delays and roadblocks than necessary. I'm glad I hung in there and trusted Him with my tailor-made route concerning my education.

Will you stay on the route God has for you? Or will you grow weary and miss out on the blessings He wants to bestow on you? Will you trust Him even when He doesn't provide you with all the answers? Will you remain faithful to His word and not try to make your own alternate route? He sees and knows all things, and He is never lacking in provision.

*The Altered Route*

"How long will your journey be? And when will you return?" the king asked Nehemiah. In response, Nehemiah gave a set time, and the king allowed him to go to Judah to rebuild it. The set time Nehemiah gave the king was not mentioned but a few chapters later, we read that Nehemiah completed what he set out to do in fifty-two days (Nehemiah 2:6; 6:52).

Back in the biblical days they didn't have all the wonderful machinery we have today to move heavy bricks and building materials. Yet Nehemiah and the Jewish people rebuilt the walls of Jerusalem that had been destroyed, in a fairly short amount of time. I'd assume that it would take at minimum two months to build such a massive wall, even with our modern-day equipment.

By walking in the favor of God, we are able to skip through some things. For example, with favor you can get a job without meeting the requirements. With favor you can buy a house without the needed credit score. When God gives you a vision, He has already made arrangements for it to manifest and He has ample provision. If you don't have

109

the money, resources, or support needed to fulfill your major assignment, that's a perfect scenario for God to show up on your behalf. God allows us to maneuver in such a way that when people look at our lives and the things we are doing, they marvel because God's hand is so evident.

This isn't a "shortcut" route but rather a "favor-cut" route. God can cut out some steps because of the favor that rests upon your life. You won't have to endure all the trials that others have had in attempting the same destination you are headed for. He will shift some things around in your favor as long as you are in His will. All this would be impossible without the strength given you by God, but with Him all things are possible.[31]

Moses, with a stuttering problem, didn't have to go through several sessions of speech therapy before he became a great speaker for God. David, a regular guy, didn't have to be born into royalty to become the king's son-in-law. The widow at Zarephath, who only had enough food for one last meal, did not have to receive government aid to feed her family. The crippled woman, who walked bent over for eighteen years, didn't have to go through years of physical therapy to be healed. These people were given alternate routes.

You don't need to look for love in all the wrong places. You don't have to receive affirmation and confirmation from people. You no longer have to worry if God will do it for you. God is giving you an alternate route.

-----------------

To me, the hardest parts of a task are starting it and completing it. Starting is difficult because you have to spend a great deal of time brainstorming and getting your ideas in order. Completing a task is difficult because you're not sure if you've covered all the necessary details.

Your navigation system will allow you to alter your route. But it won't let you delete either the first step or the last one. All of the middle can be changed, but not the most significant steps.

The past does not dictate your future. But your future is a reflection of how God can make something beautiful from your past. He leaves the beginning and finishing of a task up to us, but He will handle all that is in between, as long as we are in His will. (See Romans 5:4; James 1:3.) There you will see the importance of getting started, maintaining consistency in the middle, and crossing the finish line at the end.

*The Complete Route*

Development is a process. Along the route there will be tests and trials that exist for the purpose of building and maturing you. If you never had to cry, you wouldn't know the value of a smile. If you never felt pain, you wouldn't understand the relief that pleasure brings. If you never had to be content with little, you would not appreciate the much. There are some things God will not remove from your life, because they are fundamental assets in your maturation process.

Think about some of the things you've had to go through. What would you be like now if you hadn't experienced them? Did those things make you a better person? Did they build your faith and trust in God? Did they help you make wiser decisions later?

In the past, I've made a few bone-head decisions. But now I consult God before making a move. It's great to have that kind of testimony!

It may seem like God has whooped you time after time. But I am grateful for the "Holy Spirit spankings" I've

111

received because they set me straight. I now think twice before making a move that could be detrimental to me physically, mentally, emotionally, or spiritually.

Sometimes I wish I could've short-cut my development. But the complete route was the only path to get me to my destiny while giving me some extra things along the way, such as wisdom, knowledge, patience, stronger faith, increased reliability on God, and much more.

Joseph had to endure a long route to get where God wanted Him. He lost just about everything except his life in order to receive the double portion God had stored up for him. If he hadn't endured all that he did, he wouldn't have come to a point in his life where he was able to say, "Though He slay me, yet will I trust Him."[32]

The supreme example of someone who took the complete route is Jesus. He could have accomplished God's plan for Him in a completely different way. But He chose to follow the route the God gave Him. In the garden of Gethsemane He prayed, "My Father, if it is possible, may this cup be taken from me. Yet not as I will, but as you will"(Matthew 26:39 NIV). If there was an alternate course, He could have taken it. Yet, in the midst of His agony, He submitted to the will of the Father and willingly drank the cup that was given to Him. Now, that's taking God's perfect will to the fullest!

Because of Jesus' obedience, we are forgiven of all our sins and do not have to pay the debt we owe. Because He completed His assignment by going to the cross, we are able to be with Him eternally. I am grateful He did not choose a different path.

Remember, what you're going through is not just for you. It is also for those who see you and follow you. Don't shortchange someone else's blessing or breakthrough

112

because of your discomfort in having to go through the entire process.

## HOW WILL YOU GET TO POINT B?

The different options the GPS presents you with when you enter an address enable you to decide which way you want to travel. Do you prefer the scenic route with a lot of stops, the quickest way with minimal stops, or a blend of both scene and quickness? Each route will get you to your destination, probably within the same amount of time, give or take a few minutes. Since the time is approximately equal, the choice boils down to the specifics of how you want your journey to look.

Choosing a route isn't easy, because either one could be for your benefit or your demise. One route may look more appealing to the eye, but after you begin that journey you may find that it isn't everything you thought it was going to be. You might run into construction, roadblocks, traffic jams, or other things that slow your forward progress.

Since we are co-laborers with Christ (1 Corinthians 3:9 KJV) the choice in the path may be ours but other times He may suggest a specific one for us.

*The Expressway*

The quick route puts you on the expressway (or highway or freeway, whatever you call it). It gets you to your destination with no interruptions. Most people prefer this means of travel. But it isn't always perfect.

I often travel back and forth between Nashville and Birmingham to visit family, so the highway and I have become well acquainted. Due to my positive experiences of navigating the highway, I am quite familiar with this route. That familiarity allows for great focus, frees me to think about other things as I journey, and gives me ample space for shifting lanes.

### Great focus

While driving on the expressway, there aren't as many things you need to be observant about as there are on a busy street. You don't have to watch for pedestrians crossing or lights changing or deep potholes in the road. Your only concerns are for the other cars around you, debris in the road, and police (if you tend to be a speeder). Having only a few things to be concerned about enables you to focus on your driving.

God will give you an expressway route when He intends to get you to a place of great focus and attention. You don't have little things constantly distracting you. You are on a straightaway with a constant pace. You don't have time to look at what's going on off the expressway and you don't have the time to stop and hold conversations with those at a standstill. If they are not even remotely close to going at the same speed as you then they will ultimately slow you down.

When people are trying to stop you while at this pace, they are not realizing that if you stop, you're putting your life in danger. With cars flying past you at 70 to 80 mph, you can't just hit your brakes and stop. You'll get hurt, along with those who are in close proximity to you.

If people are trying to get your attention, you need to tell them to catch you at the next exit. But the distance between exits can vary. Some are only a mile apart, while others could be five miles or more. I'd like to assume that those times when an exit seemed far off were the times when we got antsy and wished we could find a quicker way to get off.

You don't want to try to get off the route before there's an official exit. If you drive off the expressway just because you saw something that looked appealing, you may end up in a ditch!

Many of the hurts I've had to endure have been due to trying to get off the route before there was an exit to take. Some things in life can leave you emotionally bruised and spiritually scarred. Since there wasn't an official exit, you made one on your own. You knew that relationship, that job, or that place wasn't right for you. But it looked so good at a quick glance, you jumped off and landed in the ditch.

Don't let what you see as a quick escape cause you to jump out of God's will. This will only cause more pain.

It is difficult to stay on track when there are so many things competing for your attention. But God has placed you here so He can narrow your focus and help you to stay consistent in what you need to be doing, focusing on the things He has assigned to you.

However, just because you were given an expressway route, that doesn't mean you will reach your destination more quickly. You may observe people traveling a side-street route and assume that you will arrive before they do. But their destination may be much closer than yours, so there's no need for them to get on the highway.

Don't become bitter if someone else gets to his or her destination before you reach yours. You just have a little farther to go.

### Free Thinking

Being on the highway frees you to think. On many of my long drives, the time flies by because my mind is

115

thinking about other things besides driving. I often arrive at my destination with very little recollection of the trip I just took. My body was in one place, but my mind was in another.

We may be in a terrible situation but the situation is not what He wants us to dwell on. "Brethren, whatever things are true, whatever things are noble, whatever things are just, whatever things are pure, whatever things are lovely, whatever things are of good report, if there is any virtue and if there is anything praiseworthy—meditate on these things" (Philippians 4:8). God wants you to imagine yourself out of that bad situation. If you can't see yourself out, it will be difficult for you to trust that God can make a way of escape for you.

*Being in the flow* or *being in the zone* is when people get so engulfed in what they're doing that time passes without them even noticing. You've probably experienced this if you were working on an assignment or hobby you enjoyed and looked up to find that a significant amount of time had already gone by. People that can find their *flow* or *zone* are normally happy in what they are doing. Time flies when you're having fun, right?

Wouldn't it be a blessing if you could go through a terrible storm yet still experience happiness and contentment? You can! You just need to change your thinking.

Philippians 4:8 doesn't tell us to think on whatever things are obvious, whatever is affecting you, things that are wrong. No, it says that we need to stop dwelling on the negative and find something praiseworthy to meditate on.

Perhaps your situation seems so bad that you can't come up with a single thing that is praiseworthy about it. I challenge you to open your eyes and look at the people around you.

In one of my graduate courses, my professor shared with us that one of his clients, a drug abuser, had finally stopped. When he asked her how that happened, "spirituality" was her first answer. Her second answer was "While I was in the inpatient hospital, I saw others who were worse off than I was, so I figured there was hope for me."

You'll appreciate your holey shoes when you see someone barefoot. You will appreciate your smoky car when you see someone walking. You'll appreciate your Ramen noodles when you see someone digging in the dumpster for food. And you will appreciate a break-up with your college boyfriend of three years when you see a husband and wife divorce after thirty years of marriage. Regardless of your situation, you will always be able to find something positive, even if it's only that it could be worse. When you find that something think of it often.

Shifting Room

The expressway offers you ample opportunities to maneuver and manipulate your speed. When I drive, I utilize both of these options often. Sometimes I speed up; other times I slow down. Sometimes I'm in the right lane, and sometimes in the left lane. It all depends on what I see ahead. If the car in front of me is driving slower than I desire, I change lanes to get around it. If I want to cruise, I get out of the fast lane and let others pass me. If I'm feeling heavy footed and see a police car up ahead, I slow down. If there's an open lane, I speed up.

You won't get all the way to your destination on cruise control. You will more than likely need to switch lanes a time or two.

God is not strict and rigid. He does have expectations of how things should be conducted and handled, but He disciplines and instructs in love. He knows our limitations.

There may be seasons in your life when you are "in the zone" and making good time toward your destination. Then circumstances come along and slow you down a bit. Despite the reduced speed, you are still making forward progress and getting closer to your destination.

At some points along your journey you may need to follow the cars ahead of you. At other times you might have to take the leading role. Both positions are important, because a great leader can also be led. And being able to follow with humility has its benefits.

The people who have gone ahead of you in the journey have a slight advantage because they can see a little farther ahead than you can. They will recognize a threat earlier than you and be able to provide you with a warning.

Let's say you've been cruising along the expressway. As you make your way around a winding curve in the road, you notice the cars in front of you braking. Your first response is to brake too. Seconds later you see a couple of crunched cars blocking the right lane. Because of the warning signs given by those ahead, you were able to reduce your speed and maintain your journey without getting into an accident yourself.

Now let's say you're driving and the car in front of you quickly swerves left. You do the same simply because of the other driver's reaction. Moments later you find out that both of you were maneuvering around a large piece of tire rubber, wood, or a tire-denting pothole.

The point is this. Don't get upset if God puts you behind some people you feel you should be in front of. By having you follow, He is keeping you safe from harm and danger that you wouldn't have seen otherwise, or you may have seen but not until it was too late.

*The Street Way*

Traveling via side streets may feel a little longer and more cumbersome because you have frequent stops, pedestrians in the road, and more things to focus on. It sometimes seems like every light is just waiting for you so it can turn red. And apparently every person in the entire city is headed in the same direction as you. Cars cut you off and then drive as slow as they can. You want to pick up the pace so you can get to where you need to go so this route does not seem like an ideal choice for you.

But this path isn't all bad. The side-street way gives you the opportunity to fellowship with others around you. Life isn't always about being busy and in a hurry. This route slows you down a tad so you don't neglect those around you who are important. Scripture instructs us to "not forsake the assembling of ourselves together ... but exhorting one another" (Hebrews 10:25).

I love the saying, "It's not about what you know…but who you know". The street way gives you a chance to mingle and network with those who have interests similar to yours. Maybe you'll meet people along the way who have been down the path you're on, and they can provide you with a little advice. Or maybe they've already been to where you're going, so they can offer you a hand-up to get you there.

God knows the desires of our hearts and the destinations we are pursuing, and He intentionally places people in our path as resources. Maybe you go to a meeting you really didn't want to attend, but then you discover that the guest speaker is interested in the same things you are. Or you sit angrily in the airport because your flight was delayed, but during your wait you meet someone who plays a significant role in your life later on.

Don't miss your blessing just because you don't feel like being bothered with people. In Luke 6:38 (KJV), Jesus says, "Give, and it shall be given unto you; good measure, pressed down, and shaken together, and running over, shall men give into your bosom." The people you are rolling your eyes at and ignoring could be the very ones God intends to use to bless you.

## The Back Way

The back way is the road less traveled—not due to a lack of desire but to unfamiliarity. With this route, not many people will know you are even traveling. You will reach your destination and they will stand in awe, because they thought you were doing nothing the whole time.

Sometimes God leads us to take the back way because He wants to keep us away from people and their influences for a season. It's not because He wants us to be miserable and alone. He does this so He can develop us without the criticisms of others. He wants the things we have to endure to be just between Him and us, without all the naysayers and haters along the way.

I've been on some back-road journeys, and they can get boring and lonely at times. But I can honestly say that those were the times when I was able to do a lot of work on myself. God gave me a full evaluation of myself and showed me things that needed to be removed, added, and adjusted. He plucked and pruned me so I would bear more fruit.[33]

This back-way experience can be painful, because it makes you wonder if something is wrong with you. You may find yourself asking a lot of "why" questions. *Why hasn't anyone asked me on a date? Why haven't I received a call to schedule an interview? Why didn't they accept me into that school?*

Instead of wondering what's wrong with you, look at this journey as God wanting some alone time with you.

One day, a good friend and I were chatting on the phone about singleness, and she said, "I walked past the mirror today and looked at myself and said, 'This singleness has to be a spiritual thing.'"

I laughed out loud, because she was saying that based on her outward appearance, there was no reason for her to be single.

Your current state in life has nothing to do with your looks, your credentials, or your status. God just needs to do some spiritual work on you before He can cause some things to manifest through you. He has to tweak your attitude a bit before He can make you the CEO. He's got to conduct surgery on your heart before He can send you Mr. or Ms. Right. If people ask, just tell them it's a spiritual thing.

One of the best parts about taking the back way is that when you come out, people will be shocked at your progress. They will ask how you got to the level you're at. Most important, you will be able to tell them who did it for you and offer up all the glory to God. Read Psalm 139:23–24.

*The Combo Way*

Some destinations will require you to take more than one means of travel. You may start off on the back way,

121

work your way to the street, hop onto the expressway for a while, take your exit, and do some more street or back-way driving before you arrive. Getting to your destination may not be done all in one sitting or one season. You may go through a period of aloneness, but once you've learned what you needed during that season, God may bring you back out so you can mingle with others.

Some seasons may be longer than others, but the length should not be a major consideration. Rather, focus on obtaining all of the information, knowledge, tools, and wisdom that God is trying to give you along the way. Reaching your destiny is all about moving and enduring.

## PAY ATTENTION

A GPS is only useful to the extent that the owner utilizes it. If you enter an address and then ignore everything it tells you, it serves no purpose. Likewise, if you ignore the instructions of the Holy Spirit, you are denying Him the ability to fulfill one of His purposes in your life, which is to lead, guide, and protect.

In a classroom setting, a teacher tells her students to pay attention when the information she is about to provide is material they need to know for a future test. The teacher is giving her students insight on what to expect. For the students who don't pay attention, studying will be more difficult because they didn't focus on what the teacher was saying. Typically, a teacher covers the materials that she feels is most pertinent for the students to know. Students who don't pay attention will have a harder time focusing their studies on the major points. They will aimlessly study every page rather than focusing the majority of their time on the information that was covered extensively during class.

If we do not pay attention to the instructions God gives us, we will continue to pursue life aimlessly, trying to figure out who we are and why we were placed on this earth. If we do not pay attention to what the Holy Spirit tells us, it will be difficult for us to know what to expect in our lives. We will find ourselves wondering about assignments and destinies that others have because we don't have any idea what we should be doing. We will try to live up to someone else's standards and expectations, resulting in a "measure up" complex, never being fully satisfied with who we are. If we don't pay attention, we will slowly kill ourselves.

## KNOW WHAT TO EXPECT

*Get in the Correct Lane*

Each lane serves a specific purpose for drivers. Some come to an end quickly, like those that are for entrance or exit purposes only. Some stay to the left or right, while others split down the middle and allow you to choose either way. Some are turn only, some allow you to either turn or keep straight, and some will only let you to go straight. The lane you are in has great significance because it determines the direction in which you will travel.

The different lane options signify the need to actively participate along the route. God has provided you with the destination, but it's up to you to make the necessary maneuvers and adjustments to ensure that your purpose is fulfilled.

When your GPS instructs you to make a turn and then to get into a specific lane, it is doing so to make sure you are in the right position for the next step. It also does this to ensure that you don't fall victim to the "procrastination syndrome"—waiting till the last minute to try to do something.

When my GPS tells me to merge and then keep right because my exit will be approaching soon, I get into the right lane, as instructed. But then I sometimes move back to the left lane to pass the slower cars in the right lane. I have occasionally nearly missed my exit because I was so busy trying to pass people, I didn't realize how quickly the exit was approaching.

Being in the correct lane gives you privileges that cars in different lanes don't have. One day while driving, I approached a light and got into a left lane that allowed cars to go straight or turn left. After I got into that lane, I realized that I wanted to turn right. But cars were already pulling up in the lane to my right. I couldn't go the way I wanted to because I wasn't in the proper lane. The cars in the correct lane had the privilege of turning without any restrictions.

There will be times in our lives when our Internal Navigator will give us a set of instructions and we'll put off following them. When the time comes to make something happen, we'll be unable to do so because we're in the wrong lane.

First Corinthians 14:40 says that everything needs to be done "decently and in order."

Making turns from the wrong lane is a traffic violation. Those rules are designed to protect you and other drivers. They are enforced to assure that everyone is in one accord. Imagine how chaotic streets would be if people in the left lane could turn right and cars in the right lane could turn left. What a mess that would be!

It is vital for us to do our Kingdom business decently and in order. Not stepping on anyone's toes, trying to get over people, or becoming mischievous in the ways in which we strive for success and completion of a divine assignment. If we remain in the lane we are instructed to be in, we will avoid the temptation to cut in front of someone or try to force our way back over. When things are done as they should be, there will be no need to push our way to the front or force things to happen. "What he opens no one can shut, and what he shuts no one can open" (Revelation 3:7 NIV). What God has for you is for you.

So, how do you know which lane you need to be in? If you've reached a point in your life where you feel you're doing well, staying focused and on track, but lately it seems like you've been taking a few steps backward, you may have veered off into a turning lane when you should be in the straight lane. This may have resulted when a new person came into your life. Or a new job, activity, or responsibility you took on that caused you to shift your priorities.

Or maybe you're doing one thing but feel a nudge trying to pull you in a different direction. This may indicate that you are going down the wrong path and need to make a U-turn to get back on track. For example, perhaps a job opportunity opened for you but you were uneasy about it. Or you were dating someone, and the time you spent together was enjoyable, but every time you left his or her presence you felt emptier than before. The Holy Spirit may be using those little nudges to get your attention and to lead you down a different and better path.

If you tune in to the Spirit, you will be able to discern where you should be. If you're not certain, ask yourself, *Is this thing that's pulling me in a different direction positive or negative? If I make this turn, will it be better or worse for me?* If that change would be for the better, get into the turning lane. If it will be for the worse, keep on the straight lane down the path you are currently on until you're instructed to do otherwise.

While making these decisions, keep in mind that what you consider "good" or "better" may not necessarily be God's "good" or "better" for your life. Allow the Holy Spirit to guide you safely down the path you should be on.

*Become a Discerner of Distance*

It seems the closer we get to our blessing, the more challenging our trials become. Could it be that the enemy realizes we are one step away from getting out of our circumstances and breaching the territory of the blessings that God has for us? Perhaps the enemy is thinking, *This is my last chance to get them to distrust God concerning their promise, so I need to give this blow my best shot!* The enemy sees the progress we are making, and he is not at all pleased. He is giving his all to try to set us back and to get us to doubt that God is listening to our prayers. So this is not the time to cower down! We must steady ourselves and FIGHT for our Point B! It won't just be handed to us!

The enemy is attracted to those with the anointing and favor of God on their life. For example, Job was anointed and blessed with plenty, which made him a great target for satan. As the distance between you and your destination gets smaller, the struggle may become great. This is not the time to give up, pull over and take a pit stop, or turn around. Keep trucking along and maintain your focus until you reach the end of your journey.

I'm not saying that the farther away you are from your destination, the smoother your route. But God will not give you your blessing until you're ready for it. So along the journey He is prepping and priming you. If you have a lot of stuff He needs to get out of you, you may have several bumpy roads along the way that will result in pruning, burning, and sifting. Don't lose heart. The process may hurt, but in the end you will come out as a beautiful masterpiece of God's handiwork. After all, what is a beautiful vase without the initial mashing of the clay?

I once heard someone say that if we could only get a glimpse of what God sees in our future we would be satisfied and the complaining and crying would cease. All we have to do is trust and believe that He knows what He's doing.

Along your journey you may look at your situation and think that either God isn't listening to you or He doesn't have the slightest concern about what you're going through. The opposite is true. He sees and He hears. However, He needs to know that you will trust Him regardless of your circumstances (good and bad). Satan takes one last blow right before our blessing comes. That's our final test to see if we will trust God to do what He said He will do.

I have not yet experienced giving birth to a child, but when I have watched it on television, it always seems like the final pushes are the most painful ones. Right before the baby is born, the woman feels the greatest pain. Although it seems almost unbearable, the mother must continue to push if she wants to birth her child.

You are pregnant, my friend! Your blessing is so close, you can feel it, can't you? You have been impregnated with an awesome purpose and a dynamic destiny. But how badly do you want to see it? Are you willing to push past the pain so the blessing within you can manifest itself? Or will you refuse to endure the pain and try to hold in what God has called you to release?

------------------

One day, while riding in the car with my mom, the navigation system instructed her to turn right in one hundred feet. That seemed like plenty of time. But my

127

mom said, "A hundred feet isn't very long when you're driving!"

If you are not clear on where you are in your season of life, you may do things based on an illusion of where you are rather than on reality. Illusions can cause you to become overly anxious or extremely passive and negligent when pursuing your destiny. First Corinthians 3:9 (NIV) says that we are co-workers in God's service, so He is not going to do all of the work. Discern where you are and don't use tomorrow as an excuse to not act today.

## OBEY THE INSTRUCTIONS: THE DIRECTED PATHWAY

"In all your ways acknowledge Him, and He shall direct your paths" (Proverbs 3:6). This Scripture doesn't tell us to acknowledge Him in *some* of our ways. It says *all* of our ways. Every single move we make is critical in either getting us to our destiny or pulling us away from it.

The only way you will know for sure that you are going where you need to go is to be in constant communication with the Holy Spirit. There is no shortcut around it. He desires you to have an intimate relationship with Him so He can tell you all He wants to say. Trying to find alternate ways to get the answers and guidance you need is like trying to take the Holy Spirit out of the equation. He doesn't tell us every single detail, because He wants us to come to Him for guidance, comfort, and wisdom.

At times we may get turned around, so He tells us to make a U-turn. Or maybe He wants us to collaborate with others, so He instructs us to merge with someone else. Then there are times when we need to make a sudden shift in our path, so He tells us to make a sharp turn. Let's discuss in a little more depth these ways in which we can receive guidance from the Holy Spirit.

128

*U-Turn*

"Please make a legal U-turn." This GPS instruction indicates that the direction you are going is the opposite of where you should be heading.

I've had to make some U-turns in my life. As much as I despised them at first, they were all things I had to do.

The Holy Spirit will instruct you when you get off track, but He will not drive the car for you. You have to make the decision to turn. Second Chronicles 7:14–15 says, "If My people who are called by My name will humble themselves, and pray and seek My face, and turn from their wicked ways, then I will hear from Heaven, and will forgive their sin and heal their land. Now my eyes will be open and My ears attentive to prayer made in this place." God won't make any moves on your behalf until you make the turn.

One definition of *turn* is "to convert or transform."[34] Turning doesn't mean doing a few things differently but keeping some of the old ways. It means completely altering what you're doing.

*Merge*

To *merge* means "to cause to combine or unite."[35] When your GPS instructs you to merge, it wants you to move from the lane you're in to an area where multiple lanes combine.

Merging in the spirit realm can be seen as the Holy Spirit wanting you to collaborate with another individual to make a vision or assignment happen. This merge may be temporary, or it could be a connection that will remain for a lifetime. Some examples of merges are friendships, relationships, and fellowships.

At one point in my life God moved me from being alone to "merging" with like-minded individuals who had similar passions and the same fire for Christ I had. This was one of the best times for me, because it gave me a "family" and a group of friends who would make me better.

Don't neglect the fellowship of other believers, and don't push away every person who desires to join you in your vision. God may be trying to merge the two of you together to produce greater fruit.

*Sharp Turn*

A sharp turn happens abruptly. It may not mean that you are on a wrong road. The path you're on may just need a few tweaks here and there. In the spiritual realm, I see this as an instruction to act immediately upon hearing the Holy Spirit speak, with no delays or questions.

I've experienced this when God gives me instruction through a series of dreams. A mentor of mine gave me a prophetic word one day (back when I was a "baby" in receiving and giving prophetic words), and I took what she said literally and ran with it. Little did I know that there was a procedure to be followed after receiving a word, such as testing it to see if it confirms things you already know. (If not, you put it on the shelf until you receive further instructions from God.) When I received my word, I didn't consider that there might be some symbolism in what was said. Nor did I wait for the Holy Spirit's green light.

The following week, I searched for organizations that would help me get to the place my prophecy said I should be. I found one and immediately began training to become a volunteer. Throughout the process, I felt uncertain as to whether I had correctly interpreted what God had spoken on this matter. I asked Him to show me what I should do.

The next few nights I had a couple of dreams in which the Holy Spirit instructed me to stop the training with this organization because it was not in alignment with what God had called me to do and it could potentially be harmful to me in some way (physically, emotionally, and/or spiritually). I stopped the process immediately.

Do not ignore these red flags and warning signs. They are there for a reason, and God wants you to pay attention to them.

## WARNINGS

I am grateful to God for the many ways that He chooses to speak to us. He can speak audibly, visually (in visions or dreams),[36] through others, through Scripture, and in a variety of other methods. Whatever way He chooses to communicate with us, it is important to respond accordingly as John 10:4 suggests by (1) recognizing His voice, because "His sheep know His voice" and (2) listening to what He says and obey, because "the sheep follow Him." He speaks to give us direction, correction, encouragement, comfort, and even warnings about delays, detours, roadblocks, and unexpected traffic ahead.

### Delays

I have grown to appreciate delays in my life. They can be quite annoying, but I have learned to embrace them. Delays can save you much heartache and pain. They can even save your life.

One delay potentially prevented me from being seriously injured, possibly killed. I was leaving Bible study around 6:20 PM, and I had to be somewhere at 7:00. I figured it would take me about forty minutes (plus or minus ten minutes due to traffic). I didn't want to be late, so I was antsy as I got into the car.

At the stop sign getting out of the parking lot, I ended up behind one of the church vans. It sat there for at least three minutes because traffic was coming both ways. I wanted to go around it, but there wasn't enough room. Not wanting to get agitated, I started to pray. The Holy Spirit told me to be patient because He was delaying me for a reason. That calmed me down.

When my turn finally came, I drove out of the church parking lot and headed for my next destination. I soon noticed cars in front of me slowing down. The reason: a car accident had taken place. It must have happened just a few minutes earlier, because the police hadn't arrived yet.

I was filled with joy and thanksgiving! If God had not allowed me to be stuck behind the church van for three minutes, I could have been in that accident.

When delays arise, trust that God is allowing them for your good. He sees further ahead than you do, and He makes arrangements that will benefit you in the long run. If you wait on God's timing, you will reap the benefits of trusting in Him.

### Detours and Roadblocks

Detours and roadblocks are set in place when there's something down that road that drivers do not need to be exposed to. Perhaps the concrete is disturbed due to work being done to the ground. Or construction could be taking place that could be hazardous. Power lines might be down in the middle of the road. Debris may be in the path of the drivers.

Detours and roadblocks are not intended to inconvenience drivers but rather to protect them. But they can be bothersome, especially if the detour takes you around the block, up the street, and around the corner just to get to where you were trying to go.

When the Holy Spirit puts up a roadblock in our lives, He does so to protect us from harm or danger that is in the path we are headed down. And He always provides us with a different route to assure that we don't end up lost. He provides us with detour signs that take us in a direction we may have never been before.

In a way, detours are awesome, because they teach us things we would have never been aware of otherwise. Remember, the Holy Spirit is all about guiding, directing, and teaching us. Therefore, if you find yourself at a roadblock in your life, embrace the detour, knowing He has you there for a reason. He wants to expose you to new ways of living, and to revelation and knowledge that you would never have received on your own.

*Unexpected Traffic*

Sometimes my GPS lets me know that there's heavy traffic ahead. Then I can take an earlier exit if necessary. But there are times when it doesn't warn me in advance.

Sometimes the Holy Spirit will inform you that there's something coming that will slow you down or distract you. He will allow you to take a different route around this satan-induced "traffic."

Other times, He will let you encounter slow traffic so you don't have time to get off course. He knows you won't want to slow down, even if it's necessary. Since the "slowing process" could be from God or the enemy, it's important to stay constantly connected to the Holy Spirit so you are aware of what's going on in your life.

Your heavy traffic could be God slowing you down so you don't hurt yourself and/or others. I've found this to be especially true concerning spiritual gifts. I have learned that it is better to take your time and build your character (integrity, humility, obedience, honesty, etc.) than trying to speed through that process and grow your gifting faster. If you don't have the character to support your gifting, the weight will be too heavy for you to manage and you could crumble under it. Therefore, we should embrace the seemingly slow training process.

---

### The Mental and Emotional Health Corner
#### SELF-CARE

Before I started my doctoral program, I was in a season of rest. During this time, the Lord wanted me to draw closer to Him and increase our level of intimacy so I could learn about Him on deeper levels. I was unaware that this was supposed to be a season of rest, so I continued doing everything I could. I took classes and got involved in ministries. But activity was not what He wanted me to be doing at that moment.

In a series of dreams, God told me to "slow my roll." Then one morning, He told my mom to tell me I needed to slow down. I was trying to move ahead of God, and the Holy Spirit was telling me to embrace my "traffic season." That was difficult for me, because I'm so used to going and doing. I am an initiator that likes to always make things happen. Being given permission to rest was a new thing for me.

We all need these seasons to be rejuvenated. If we miss out on them, we will overwork ourselves and get burnt out. Therefore, self-care does not need to be an after thought but rather forethought. How do you take care of yourself on a consistent basis? Need some good ideas? Google : Self-Care Wheel and you will find plenty of ideas to choose from.

---

Now, there is a difference between being in a rest season and just being lazy and not wanting to do anything. If God is telling you to pick up the pace, do a self-check and see what areas in your life the enemy is taking hold of to cause you to be disobedient to God's instructions to get busy. Proverbs 24:30–34 and Ecclesiastes 10:18 clearly show us the results of being lazy.

------------------

In my book Owning Possible I talk about paying attention to the warnings and how to get 20/20 foresight instead of 20/20 hindsight. I discussed how many times we don't think we received a warning from the Lord before something bad happened to us. But often, after the bad thing happens, we say, "I knew I shouldn't have done that" or "I knew I shouldn't have talked to them." Looking back, you acknowledge that uneasy feeling you got. The Holy Spirit always provides us with warnings when something isn't right.

Of course, hindsight is always 20/20. But I want to encourage you to listen to God's warnings. Then you can have 20/20 foresight! If you heed the lack-of-peace signs, and obey His promptings, you can avoid many negative things in life.

We often overlook these warnings because they aren't what we want to be true. But in the end we wish we'd listened. I am sure the person who married someone who they were warned not to or the person who invested all of their money into something that they were not supposed to can testify to this. You can avoid many mistakes by cleaning out your spiritual ears and eyes and seeing life and circumstances from Heaven's perspective. You will never go wrong with this outlook!

1. What investments have you made into your destiny? What have you done to symbolize your seriousness and commitment to fulfilling your purpose in life?
2. If you had to choose a route to describe where you currently are which would you choose and why? What are your feelings about the particular route that you are on (Content, unsatisfied, indifferent…)?
3. What other routes have you been on in your journey? How would you describe your experience in each different journey? What did you learn differently?
4. Have you experienced any setbacks or progress on your journey? Discuss.
5. Read Psalms 25:9, 12 and 107:30. How can you apply these Scriptures to your life?
6. We talked about being able to have *free thinking* when on the expressway. How would you describe your thinking as it pertains to your life, trials you face, and your destiny?
7. How could you improve your thinking to be more optimistic?
8. Read Romans 9:20–21. How can you use this Scripture during those times when you want to question God and His agenda for your life?
9. Do you recall a time when God warned you about something but you ignored it? If you could change that decision, would you? What would you have done differently?

# STEP SIX

## ARRIVE AT YOUR DESTINATION

### MAKE THE TRIP WORTH YOUR WHILE

*Take a Glance Back*

While on a road trip, it is important to utilize our car's windows and mirrors. The windshield is larger than the mirrors for a reason: you should be spending more time looking ahead than looking back. The mirrors help you shift lanes as you continue to move forward.

A proper perspective of the past enables us to acknowledge what has happened to us. But we only stay there long enough to help us make forward progress. Our past should not dictate our future. But our perspectives and attitudes about what has happened can determine the direction that we will go.

If you look back and are bitter, angry, and revengeful, this negative reflection will stall your forward progress. However, if you recognize that some things didn't happen the way you would have liked yet you are able to forgive, let it go, and move on, this will enhance your forward progress.

Dwelling on what has happened can become a hindrance to what is and what shall be. However, ignoring the past isn't beneficial either. Isaiah 43:18's admonition to "not remember the former things" does not mean we should develop a severe case of amnesia. The prophet is suggesting that we not focus on what has been. The rest of the verse says, "Do not dwell on the past. See, I am doing a new thing! Now it springs up; do you not perceive it? I am making a way in the desert and streams in the wasteland." God wants to give us a fresh perspective while we're in our current situation. If we are stuck looking back, we will miss what He wants to show us.

We should look back long enough to remember, lest we forget where God has brought us from, and long enough for the past to become engrained in us so we don't repeat the same mistakes, but not so long that the past causes us to lose focus on the present and the future.

*Review*

Proverbs 3:1–2 (NIV) says, "My son, do not forget my teaching, but keep my commands in your heart, for they will prolong your life many years and bring you peace and prosperity."

I once had a dream that I desired to obtain a higher degree in education, but before I could I had to go through high school again. I didn't need to repeat all of my classes, but I had to review some things before I could move ahead. In this dream I forgot the combination to my locker. But the principal gave me the key so I could open my locker and get my combination, which was written on my agenda inside the locker.

After I awoke from this dream, God pointed me to Proverbs 3:1. The message that I received from this verse was for me to take the time to look back at all the things I had already learned and to store them in my heart so that I would not forget them. He also spoke to me through a friend who instructed me to treasure all of the new revelations God had given me and to not forget any of them.

In my dream, high school represented the Holy Spirit. (Both have the same initials.) Before God could propel me to a higher level, I had to reflect on everything He had already taught me—all of the wisdom and revelation He had provided me with thus far.

When you're in school, it is important to remember the things that you learn in your classes, especially the ones that are prerequisites for other classes. Because they build on one another, forgetting the previous information would be counterproductive.

The school of the Holy Spirit is the same way. He doesn't want us to go through an experience and then forget everything we learned from it. He wants us to remember so the early lessons can help us with subsequent levels.

Reflecting on everything you've learned in each season is like reviewing the material before taking the test that qualifies you to graduate to the next grade. If you don't pass the tests, you will have to either retake them or repeat the grade. So pay attention, remember the lessons, and live accordingly.

Each test in every season should bring you more wisdom and understanding.

*Blessed are those who find wisdom,*
*those who gain understanding,*
*for she is more profitable than silver*
*and yields better returns than gold.*
*She is more precious than rubies;*
*nothing you desire can compare with her.*

*Long life is in her right hand;*
*in her left hand are riches and honor.*
*Her ways are pleasant ways,*
*and all her paths are peace.*
*She is a tree of life to those who take hold of her;*
*those who hold her fast will be blessed.*
Proverbs 3:13–18 (NIV)

Gaining and using wisdom will prevent you from making poor decisions. It also keeps you from wasting time, thus providing you with a long and peaceful life.

## OWN UP TO YOUR PART

The hardest part about reflecting over our journey is owning the part we played; especially owning the not so pretty parts. "When I was a child, I spoke as a child, I understood as a child, I thought as a child; but when I became a man, I put away childish things" (1 Corinthians 13:11). I love this Scripture, because it eradicates all excuses for irresponsibility. When you're a child you can get away with just about anything, but when you are deemed an adult you are cut very little slack. As you get older and experience life more, you are expected to take on more responsibility and conduct yourself as an adult should. Society holds you accountable for your actions.

That same expectation applies to us spiritually too.

Many people blame satan, evil spirits, other people, the government, etc. for how they conduct themselves and why they cannot succeed in life. I'm not saying that satan doesn't put up roadblocks. He does. Nor am I saying that evil spirits don't exist. They do. But when will we start taking responsibility for what has happened in our lives?

Let's get out of the "woe is me" and "I'm the victim" mentality. In most circumstances we determine what we
140

will think, how we will respond, and what we will do about the matters in our lives.

It's easy to play the blame game and point the finger. But that changes nothing about your situation. You will still be in the same predicament you were in prior to complaining.

If you want to accomplish all the great things God has planned for you, begin taking responsibility for your actions, your laziness, your diligence, your procrastination, your level of effort and commitment. When you are pursuing your destiny, excuses should be excommunicated! Remember, getting from point A to point B is all about being pro-active and anti-lazy.

Paul reminds us of the responsibility and accountability believers in Christ must have:

> *What shall we say then? Shall we continue in sin that grace may abound? Certainly not! How shall we who died to sin live any longer in it? Or do you not know that as many of us as were baptized into Christ Jesus were baptized into His death? Therefore we were buried with Him through baptism into death, that just as Christ was raised from the dead by the glory of the Father, even so we also should walk in newness of life. For if we have been united together in the likeness of His death, certainly we also shall be in the likeness of His resurrection, knowing this, that our old man was crucified with Him, that the body of sin might be done away with, that we should no longer be slaves of sin. For he who has died has been freed from sin. Now if we died with Christ, we believe that we shall also live with Him, knowing that Christ, having been raised from the dead, dies no more. Death no longer has dominion over Him. For the death that He died, He died to sin once for all; but the life that He lives, He lives to God. Likewise you also, reckon yourselves to be dead indeed to sin, but alive to God in Christ Jesus our Lord.*
> *Romans 6:1–11*

There are times when we mess up and don't do everything we could have done. But that should not be a pattern. We should be making every effort to walk the strait and narrow path (Matthew 7:14).

## EMBRACE YOUR SUCCESS

When you do reach your destination, celebrate! When I accomplish a major goal or task, I reward myself. It's okay to pat yourself on the back once in a while. We have to encourage ourselves as David did in I Samuel 30:6.

The accomplishment of a season can be something tangible, like a diploma, a new job, or a new business. Or it could be something intangible, such as spiritual or emotional growth. Regardless of the destination, every journey requires guidance from the Holy Spirit.

Keep in mind that God is ever moving, so the conclusion to one season in life is always the beginning of another.

## HOW DO YOU KNOW YOU'VE ARRIVED?

When you've accomplished something in the physical realm, the sign of your success is often obvious. You walk across a stage to receive your diploma. You get that promotion. Your marriage is back on track. You make the team.

Emotional and spiritual arrivals are less obvious because growth in these areas occurs on a continuous basis. We will always have room for improvement and change but if we look closely, we can recognize signs that healing and/or maturation has taken place. Since physical arrivals are more concrete, we will discuss emotional and spiritual arrivals here.

You will notice a difference in a specific area of your life. Sometimes others will notice too.

For example, if you've struggled with depending on a man or woman to validate and affirm you at all times, a good sign that you've grown past that is when you no longer seek out the approval of others to feel your worth and value. You now find complete satisfaction in the Lord, and you exude confidence in your identity in Christ.

Or let's say you've been hurt in several relationships. Maybe it started with your parents, then happened in friendships, and even intimate relationships. These experiences have made you bitter, cynical, frustrated, and leery of new people. A sign of progress in your journey of being freed from those bondages would be your ability to forgive those who've wronged you, seeing them without rage bubbling up inside you, and the ability to form securely attached relationships.

You will know when you have arrived when those things that once bound you no longer have control over your life.

This will continue to be a process. When the enemy gets kicked out of a place, he will come back, along with some of his buddies, and try to crash the place.[38] So make sure your spiritual house is cleaned up and all the rooms are filled with the Holy Spirit so there will be no room for the enemy to come back and take up residence again. Let the Holy Spirit guide you in this deliverance process, and ask Him to put people in your path that can help you.

### Christ Focused

If you are focusing on things and people around you, you may feel like you haven't truly arrived. "Success" doesn't look or feel like you expected it to. And people may not applaud you as you cross the finish line.

Just because you don't have cheerleaders on the sideline, that doesn't mean you haven't reached your destination. Not everybody is going to be ecstatic about your accomplishments and the healthy changes that have taken place in your life. But if you stay focused on Christ, the negative factors will appear minimal to you.

---

### The Mental and Emotional Health Corner
#### EMOTIONAL INTELLIGENCE

One sure sign that you have reached a whole new level mentally and emotionally is the increase in your Emotional Intelligence (EQ). You know your EQ has increased when your emotions are no longer in the driver seat. You don't let fear, anxiety, depression, or any irrational feeling or thought steer you in the wrong direction. Instead, you are able to take a step back from your situation and look at the bigger picture. You also make much more sound and rational decisions. You aren't driven by impulsive urges to quickly move out of an uncomfortable state. You also know your EQ has increased when you have a better understanding of other's emotions as well. You are able to step into another person's shoes, empathize with them, agree to disagree when needed, and provide compassion when necessary. You know your EQ has increased when the tug of war between your heart and mind lessons. This doesn't mean it disappears because it is normal to weigh the voice of your thoughts against the voice of your feelings. Each can provide you with vital content when utilized properly. Finally, I define EQ as reaching that place of mental and emotional rest where peace lives and where you simply learn to just FLOW with life. Not resisting and not forcing things to happen/not to happen.

You may find yourself on the same journey multiple times. God wants us to get all the knowledge, wisdom, and revelation He intends for us to have. If you've rushed through a particular season, or if you made it through but found yourself going back to the same place you started, you may be experiencing a "repeat journey."

Christ is persistent! Just when we think we've slipped past Him, He politely taps us on the shoulder and whispers, *I'm not done with you yet.*

In a video game, if you get halfway through and are doing poorly, you can press Restart. Or if you get to the end and your performance wasn't your best, you can push Replay. I've had a few restarts and replays in my life. Are they fun? Nah. Are they worth it? Absolutely. Because I needed all the information that "level 1" provided me to sustain me at "level 10."

## EMBRACE YOUR NEW SEASON

Once you hear, "you have reached your destination", what do you do next? First, you be sure you're really at the correct location. Then, you find a parking spot and get out of the car.

When the Holy Spirit gives us the signal that we've reached our destination, He wants us to get out, stretch (lift our hands and open our mouths to give Him praise), and embrace the destiny He has brought us to. Show your appreciation for how He kept you through the journey by dwelling in the place He has brought you to.

When you set out on a road trip, you don't enter a location into your GPS, drive to where it leads you, then

145

immediately turn back around. You get out and take care of business at that location.

Don't just accept what God has promised you and then throw it all away by reverting to your old ways and going back to what you're used to. The end of one season is an invitation to the next. Christ always moves forward, and so should you.

If we sit for too long, we will become complacent at the level we are in. So don't get so comfortable where you are that when God asks you to move you resist.[39] Make up your mind to embrace your new situation, forget about the old one, and continue to press ahead.[40]

## Manage What You've Been Given

Jesus' parable of the talents[41] teaches us the importance of being good stewards of what He gives us and how to be fruitful and multiply whatever He entrusts to us.[42] God never gives with the intentions of us hogging it all for ourselves. As we are receiving, we should also be giving.[43] Don't be like the servant who was given one talent and hid what he was given. In the end, he lost it.[44]

## Appreciate the Naysayers

This may come as a shocker to you, but not everybody is going to be excited about your success. Some may appear happy, but deep down they're not. Some may actually express disdain over your accomplishments, either to your face or to others behind your back. But this is nothing to fret about. "The LORD said to my Lord, 'Sit at My right hand, till I make your enemies your footstool.'"[45] So essentially, your haters are your elevators.

People often envy what others have, even though they're too lazy to put in the work and effort it takes to get it. And they hate it when others surpass them in their stuck,

146

mediocre state. If you're not moving, you won't have haters. The more progressive you are, the more you will intimidate and frustrate those who are stagnant. But don't worry. Consider them confirmation that you are doing wonderful works for the Lord!

1. When you look back over your life, how do you feel about the many choices and decisions you have made?

2. What lessons have you learned that have stuck with you? Although they may have been painful, would you say you are better because of them? Explain.

3. What would you tell someone who is going through a similar situation now?

4. What season are you currently in? Are you handling it effectively? Explain.

5. Who has had a direct influence on your life because of the story he/she shared with you about his/her encounters with Jesus Christ?

6. When it comes to sharing your testimony, are you honest, transparent, and 100 percent real? If not, why are you holding back? (Remember, shame and guilt are not from God.)

# STEP SEVEN

## HELP SOMEBODY WALK THROUGH THE JOURNEY YOU JUST ENDURED AND PREPARE FOR MORE

### WITNESS TO OTHERS ABOUT YOUR STORY

Our life journeys don't end. Just when you think you've figured it all out, God does something that makes you wonder.

In 2011, a few friends traveled to Redding, California, for an Open Heavens Conference at Bethel Church, where Bill Johnson is the senior pastor. After the conference, they talked excitedly about how God's glory fell in that place. Healings took place, miracles happened, and lives were changed.

I longed to experience that for myself. I appreciated the testimony of my friends, but I wanted to see it all with my own eyes![46]

Even secondhand, that testimony affected my perspective on life. I began to see changes that needed to take place in my spiritual life, and my gifts were stirred up. I'd thought I was at a good point in my relationship with Christ, but oh did He have more to show me! My eyes and ears were opened to new revelations and visions. My heart began to burn more for God.[37] I needed more and I desired more like never before.

My friends' testimonies started me on a new journey. My purpose in life became clearer and my focus was altered. What I thought I was supposed to be doing was much smaller than what God intended. This testimony opened me up to receive *all* of God's will.

So when you think you know it all and have accomplished it all, just wait. There's more to come!

I have never been as hungry for God or on fire for Christ as I am now. This journey is new for me, and I love every bit of it. I'm learning things about the Lord that I never understood. And I'm discovering things about my authority and power that I wasn't fully aware of. It's almost as if I'm a babe in Christ all over again. I feel like a kid in a candy store.

Every new thing He shows me and tells me sends a stimulating surge through my body. Just when I think I've figured Him out, He says, "Wait. There's more of Me and more of you that I want to expose you to. Come, walk with Me." My goal now is to seek Him with all of my being, to increase in intimacy with Him, and to dwell with Him and He with me.

I encourage you to share the testimonies of your life journey. Tell others how God is revealing Himself to you. The end of your journey can spark the beginning of another person's. So open your mouth and share the goodness of the Lord and how He has worked through your life in your seasons. Believe me, someone is listening. And someone is gleaning. "For the testimony about Jesus is essentially the prophetic spirit" (Revelation 19:10 The Voice).

# YOUR ROUTE GUIDANCE IS NOW FINISHED

After the navigational device tells you that you've reached your destination, it says one last thing. "Your route guidance has now finished." You won't hear anything else from it until you program in a new destination.

The Holy Spirit is not like that. God is progressive, so He won't allow you to stay in one place forever. After all, there's always room to mature and expand.

You never know when it will be time for you to "hit the road" again. So be sure to have your "spiritual listening" turned on at all times so you can receive the Holy Spirit's "alert" when it's time to begin your next journey.

## WELCOME TO POINT B

We've all achieved times of success in our lives. Some are miniature; others may be grand. Whether it's getting a driver's license, passing a class, getting a job, winning a competition, publishing your first book, or being picked on a team, one word pops into your head. *Finally!* You trained, studied, worked, cried, clawed, scratched, pressed, endured, and overcame, and now you let out a sigh of relief.

*Finally* is a joyous word, because it vividly depicts the time, effort, energy, and emotions you poured out. The wait seemed to last forever, but what you desired has come! Your hopes have turned into actuality, and your natural eyes now see what you saw only by faith. The thing you've been praying and believing God for has happened! That's a great feeling, isn't it?

Thoroughly enjoy your "finally" moments. Be grateful for the journey, and give God all the glory, because without Him you wouldn't have been able to endure the hardships you experienced on the way, and you wouldn't have reached your place of destiny. You've worked long and hard, so take a moment to celebrate and relax.

Maintain diligence and progressiveness throughout your life, regardless of the assignment. And remember that your tomorrows will always turn into yesterdays if you don't act today.

When you become an initiator you will always be proactive and anti-lazy. Don't wait for things to happen. Make things happen.

| The Mental and Emotional Health Corner |
|---|

PSYCHOLOGICAL HARDINESS

It takes psychological hardiness to finish what you start! If you've ever completed any major task you know what I am talking about. It takes a mental toughness topped with resiliency and determination to reach your end goal. Point B's aren't for the weak and feeble. It's for those that know how to close the deal. Those with psychological hardiness also are committed to the task at hand and won't stop until the work is complete. Are you psychologically tough or do you crumble at the slightest sign of adversity and challenge? I don't want to sound like a drill Sargent, but if you do feel psychologically weak, toughen up. I understand what it's like to have setbacks and to feel like you were handed the short end of the stick but those who are psychologically hardy don't let circumstances become their excuses for inaction.

## ✠ *Food For Thought* ✠

1. How do you plan to honor the Father for the many things He has brought you through and to?
2. Evaluate your progress on your current assignment. How are you doing?
3. What areas in your life still need fine-tuning and pruning?
4. Evaluate your relationship with the Father. Do you see areas where you have been slacking? How can this relationship be improved?
5. What "Point Bs" has the Holy Spirit helped you obtain in the past? How can you use these as faith builders, reminding yourself that if He did it before He can do it again?

# CHAPTER NOTES

### Preface to the Second Edition

1. Joseph Warren Walker III is the senior pastor at Mount Zion Baptist Church in Nashville, Tennessee.

2. I tend to use the words *promise, purpose,* and *assignment* interchangeably. But *promise* refers specifically to those things that God has spoken over our lives that will come to pass. *Purpose* refers to the lifetime assignments placed on us (e.g., teaching, preaching, evangelizing). *Assignment* refers to a goal or task (such as writing a book or starting a business) that God has instructed us to fulfill. Your assignments are the puzzle pieces that make up your overall purpose.

### Step One- Familiarize Yourself with Your Internal Navigator

3. "Man who is born of woman is of few days and full of trouble" (Job 14:1).

4. Discussion of being born again can be found in John 3:1–21.

5. "GPS Car Navigation System," *Electronics Information Online,* 2006, http://www.electronics-manufacturers.com/info/satellite-communications/gps-car-navigation-system.html.

6. This is a joke that has been told for years and in many versions. The author is unknown.

7. Ephesians 1:11 (NIV).

8. According to BibleStudyTools.com (Salem Web Network, 2013), a *rhema* word is a word "that is or has been uttered by the living voice". So essentially it is a relevant word spoken into your right-now situation.

9. GPS Car Navigation System," *Electronics Information Online,* 2006, http://www.electronics-manufacturers.com/info/satellite-communications/gps-car-navigation-system.html.

10. "GPS Car Navigation System," *Electronics Information Online,* 2006, http://www.electronics-manufacturers.com/info/satellite-communications/gps-car-navigation-system.html.

## Step Two- Address any Distractions and Barriers Before Getting Started

11. Mark 12:30.

12. Galatians 6:2.

13. Iris Beneli. *Selective Attention and Arousal.* 1997. http://www.csun.edu/~vcpsy00h/students/arousal.htm.

## Step Three- Identify Your Point A: Where are you now?

14. "For God is not a God of disorder but of peace" (1 Corinthians 14:33 NIV).

15. "Promotion cometh neither from the east, nor from the west, nor from the south. But God is the judge: he putteth down one, and setteth up another" (Psalm 75:6–7 KJV).

16. "Death and life are in the power of the tongue, and those who love it will eat its fruit" (Proverbs 18:21).

17. "For the gifts and the calling of God are irrevocable" (Romans 11:29).

18. "But as for you, you meant evil against me; but God meant it for good, in order to bring it about as it is this day, to save many people alive" (Genesis 50:20). "And we know that all things work together for good to those who love

God, to those who are the called according to His purpose" (Romans 8:28).

19. Jonah 1–3.
20. Corey, G. *Theory and Practice of Counseling and Psychotherapy* (Belmont, CA: Thomas Brooks/Cole, 2009), 236.
21. Philippians 1:6.
22. See Appendix.
23. Psalm 51.
24. James 4:8.

## Step Four- Identify Your Point B: Where do you want to go?

25. Jeremiah 29:11 (NIV).
26. Hebrews 11:1.
27. Proverbs 3:5.
28. Genesis 22:2 is a great Bible example of this principle.

## Step Five- Prepare for the Stuff in Between Point A and Point B

29. *The New Strong's Concise Concordance & Vine's Concise Dictionary of the Bible.* (Nashville, TN: Thomas Nelson, Inc, 1999), 133.
30. Bishop T.D. Jakes, "Tap Your Treasure." Sermon at the Threshing Floor Revival, Atlanta, GA, 2006.
31. Matthew 19:26.
32. Job 13:15.
33. John 15:2.
34. Merriam-Webster Online," *Merriam-Webster Inc.* 2013,http://www.merriam-webster.com/dictionary/turn.
35. "Merriam-Webster Online," *Merriam-Webster Inc.* 2013,http://www.merriam-webster.com/dictionary/merge.

36. A suggested book is *Dream Language: The Prophetic Power of Dreams, Revelations, and the Spirit of Wisdom* by James Goll (Destiny Image Publishers, 2006).

### Step Six- Arrive at Your Destination

37. "Then I said, 'I will not make mention of him, nor speak anymore in His name.' But His word was in my heart like a burning fire shut up in my bones; I was weary of holding it back, and I could not" (Jeremiah 20:9).
38. Matthew 12:43–45.
39. "Behold, I will do a new thing; now it shall spring forth; shall you not know it? I will even make a road in the wilderness and rivers in the desert" (Isaiah 43:19).
40. "Brethren, I count not myself to have apprehended: but this one thing I do, forgetting those things which are behind, and reaching forth unto those things which are before, I press toward the mark for the prize of the high calling of God in Christ Jesus" (Philippians 3:13–14 KJV).
41. Matthew 25:14–30.
42. "And God blessed them, and God said unto them, Be fruitful, and multiply, and replenish the earth, and subdue it: and have dominion over the fish of the sea, and over the fowl of the air, and over every living thing that moveth upon the earth" (Genesis 1:28 KJV).
43. "Heal the sick, cleanse the lepers, raise the dead, cast out demons. Freely you have received, freely give" (Matthew 10:8).
44. Matthew 25:14–30.
45. Acts 2:34–35.

## Step Seven- Help Somebody Walk Through the Journey You Just Endured and Prepare for More

46. "So then faith cometh by hearing, and hearing by the word of God" (Romans 10:17 KJV). "And they overcame him by the blood of the Lamb, and by the word of their testimony; and they loved not their lives unto the death" (Revelation 12: 11 KJV).

# ABOUT THE AUTHOR

Trillion Small has a Ph.D. in Clinical Counseling and is an adjunct professor at the University of Texas at Dallas in the Behavioral and Brain Sciences Department. She is a Licensed Marriage and Family Therapist and is a certified John Maxwell Leadership Coach. She is the CEO of Attachment Leadership, LLC where she provides the following services:

- Customized Leadership Development Programs
- Emotional Intelligence Corporate Training
- Youth Development Curriculum
- Trauma Focused Therapy

**Stay Connected:**
Instagram, Facebook, Twitter, Youtube : @TrillionSmall
Contact me for speaking, training, or counseling inquiries: www.trillionsmall.com

## WANT TO WALK YOUR GROUP THROUGH THESE 7 STEPS?

You can also find the facilitators guide for this book on my website.

# APPENDIX

*Then Peter said unto them, Repent, and be baptized every one of you in the name of Jesus Christ for the remission of sins, and ye shall receive the gift of the Holy Ghost. (Acts 2:38 KJV)*

*"The word is near you; it is in your mouth and in your heart" that is, the message concerning faith that we proclaim: If you declare with your mouth, "Jesus is Lord," and believe in your heart that God raised Him from the dead, you will be saved. For it is with your heart that you believe and are justified, and it is with your mouth that you profess and are saved. (Romans 10:8–10 NIV)*

## Prayer to receive Jesus Christ as your personal Savior:

Dear Lord Jesus, I desire to have a more intimate relationship with You. I desire to give my entire life to You. So I ask You to forgive me of all my sins and make me whole. I believe in my heart that God raised You from the dead, and I confess with my mouth that You are Lord. Come into my heart now and be my Savior. I desire to be a better person, so I will mark this day as the first day of my new journey walking with You. Thank You for saving me!

Lord God, I ask You to cover me and keep me protected as I begin to draw closer to You. I am aware that the enemy will not like this decision I have made, but I know I am safe in Your arms. Thank You for shielding me, and thank You for helping me to maintain my new focus on You. I will make You greater and all of my problems smaller. I am grateful for Your forgiveness, and I forgive myself as well as anyone I need to forgive. I am starting fresh with a new slate today, Lord!

Thank You, Father, for saving me. In Jesus' name, amen.

If you just said that prayer for the first time, welcome to the family of believers! I am very happy that you took the first step. This is the best decision you could have made in your life. God is with you. So continue pressing forward from here and don't look back.

### Here are a few suggestions for your continued growth in the Lord:

- Find a Bible-based church where you can learn the Word. Faith comes by hearing the Word of God (Romans 10:17).
- Find like-minded people to connect with, those who are going in the same direction you are now. This will be great for accountability.
- Stay encouraged. The enemy does not appreciate you "changing teams" on him, so expect him to respond. But you have nothing to fear. God is with you, and He is greater than your enemies and anything you may go through.
- The past is the past, so leave it there.
- Celebrate this awesome time of your life!